Cambridge Elements

Elements in Translation and Interpreting
edited by
Kirsten Malmkjær
University of Leicester

THE GRAECO-ARABIC TRANSLATION MOVEMENT

El-Hussein A. Y. Aly
Indiana University

CAMBRIDGE
UNIVERSITY PRESS

CAMBRIDGE
UNIVERSITY PRESS

Shaftesbury Road, Cambridge CB2 8EA, United Kingdom

One Liberty Plaza, 20th Floor, New York, NY 10006, USA

477 Williamstown Road, Port Melbourne, VIC 3207, Australia

314–321, 3rd Floor, Plot 3, Splendor Forum, Jasola District Centre,
New Delhi – 110025, India

103 Penang Road, #05–06/07, Visioncrest Commercial, Singapore 238467

Cambridge University Press is part of Cambridge University Press & Assessment,
a department of the University of Cambridge.

We share the University's mission to contribute to society through the pursuit of education, learning and research at the highest international levels of excellence.

www.cambridge.org
Information on this title: www.cambridge.org/9781009385602

DOI: 10.1017/9781009385626

First published 2023

A catalogue record for this publication is available from the British Library.

ISBN 978-1-009-38560-2 Paperback
ISSN 2633-6480 (online)
ISSN 2633-6472 (print)

The Graeco-Arabic Translation Movement

Elements in Translation and Interpreting

DOI: 10.1017/9781009385626
First published online: June 2023

El-Hussein A. Y. Aly
Indiana University

Author for correspondence: Hanan Mousa, hananaly2003@yahoo.com

Abstract: To encompass the history of the Arabic practice of translation, this Element redefines translation as combination, that is, a process of meaning-remaking that synthesizes multiple realities. The Arabic translators of the Middle Ages did not simply find an equivalent to the source text but combined its meaning with their own knowledge and experience. Thus, part of translating a text was to add new thought to it. It implies a complex process that Homi Bhabha calls "cultural hybridity," in which the target text combines knowledge of the source text with knowledge from the target culture, with the source text being different from the target text "without assumed or imposed hierarchy." Arabic translations were a cultural hybridity because the translators added new thought to their target texts, and because they saw their language as equal to Greek.

Keywords: Arabic approach to translation, translation history, Graeco-Arabic translation, translation definitions, Arabic language

ISBNs: 9781009385602 (PB), 9781009385626 (OC)
ISSNs: 2633-6480 (online), 2633-6472 (print)

Contents

1 Introduction: Toward a New Definition of Translation

The Arabic translation that occurred during the Middle Ages has played a more effective role in transforming the Arabic culture than contemporary translation theory and practice, and is entirely worthy of careful and detailed description. The Arabic translators of the Middle Ages did not simply render the meanings of source texts, but they critically and creatively engaged with them. That is to say, translation was not a means of knowledge transfer where equivalence was the major priority, but rather was a tool for knowledge production whose main purpose was applying knowledge and adding to it. As Uwe Vagelpohl states, "The texts produced during the Greek-Arabic translation movement are independent literary facts: they are based on Greek and/or Syriac source texts but they often enough put forward arguments and make points which differ from what we would expect on the basis of our carefully collated and thoroughly annotated and researched editions."[1]

The translators began a tradition of engaging critically with their source texts, adding new thought to them, which the Muslim scholars developed further in original composition. The most fascinating outcome of this approach was the transformation of the Arabic language, turning it into an ideal medium for the advancement of philosophy and science. In fact, the precision of some of the translated terms "even surpassed that of the original Greek texts," so they became the model for the western languages when these texts were later translated into Latin. In addition to the transformation of the Arabic language, the Arabic approach to translation helped create whole new disciplines such as Islamic philosophy. Using the philological outlook, which emerged only recently in modern Europe, as a paradigm to analyze and assess Arabic translation would reduce the Graeco-Arabic translation movement to the preservation of Greek knowledge until it was rediscovered in Europe, which is not the full story of Arabic translation. Thus, a proper description of the Graeco-Arabic translation movement needs to begin with a redefinition of translation, since traditional definitions are not comprehensive enough to encompass the history of Arabic translation.

Surveying the history of science translation in the Roman, Syriac, Indian, Pahlavi, and Arabic traditions in the premodern world, Scott Montgomery defines translation as "the process of transforming a specific piece of one language (commonly a text of some sort) into another language."[2] Two words

[1] Uwe Vagelpohl. *Aristotle's Rhetoric in the East: The Syriac and Arabic Translation and Commentary Tradition* (Leiden: Brill, 2008), p. 209.

[2] Scott Montgomery. *Science in Translation: Movements of Knowledge Through Cultures and Time* (Chicago: University of Chicago Press, 2000), p. 4.

are significant in this definition: process and transformation. The word "process" implies an ongoing activity, so the target text is tentative, fluid, and in constant movement. The word "transformation" implies a complex process that Homi Bhabha calls "cultural hybridity."[3] There are two features of this cultural hybridity. First, the target text is not a copy of the source text; it combines knowledge of the source text with knowledge from the target culture. Second, the source text is different from the target text "without assumed or imposed hierarchy."[4] This applies to Arabic translation in the Middle Ages. Arabic translations were a cultural hybridity because the translators added new thought to their target texts, and because, unlike the Roman translators who saw the Greek texts as masterpieces to imitate, they saw their language as equal to the Greek language and capable of expressing scientific ideas. They did not imitate and displace the Greek texts. They acknowledged them, but also corrected and improved them.

In order to account for the history of the practice of Arabic translation, I define translation as combination, that is, a process of remaking meaning that synthesizes multiple realities. The Arabic translators of the Middle Ages did not simply find an equivalent to the source text but combined its meaning with the target language, culture, and sociopolitical context. In addition, Arabic translators combined knowledge from the source text with their own knowledge and experience. Thus, part of translating a text was to add new thought to it. A translation did not simply communicate the original meaning but improved it. To distinguish the source text from the added parts, these new parts were written in different or thicker ink, introduced in separate sections, or marked with phrasal verbs that identified the author. The addition of original composition and thought ensured the utmost critical and creative engagement with the source text and set translation on a par with writing.

However, translation as combination does not fully explain the success of the Graeco-Arabic translation movement. Accompanying this feature is another that I call the "spiral of influence."[5] The spiral of influence explains how translation enriched the Arabic language and turned it into the language of science. For example, when a term was introduced through translation, it moved up the spiral. That is, once the term was introduced, more scholars, then more people from the masses, began to use it. Therefore, it became part of Arabic language, culture, and daily life. Such an upward movement was contingent upon an environment in which more scholars and more people from the masses

[3] Homi K. Bhabha. *The Location of Culture* (London: Routledge, 1994), p. 2.

[4] Bhabha, *The Location of Culture*, p. 4.

[5] See also El-Hussein A. Y. Aly. *Qur'ān Translation as a Modern Phenomenon* (Leiden: Brill, 2023).

could engage in science. If that was not the case, it would be difficult for the term to enter common usage. It would probably confine itself to the discourse of the elite or fade away altogether. It was also possible that a term could move down the spiral after its introduction because it was not optimal enough and, in this case, a new term was usually introduced to replace it. The spiral of influence also explains the failure of translation in the contemporary Arab world, since its upward movement is too slow, given the high level of illiteracy.

My investigation relies on three sources. First, the statements put out by the Muslim scholars in the Middle Ages about translation are useful, even though they are too sporadic, brief, and general to lay the foundation for a theory. Second, more recently Graeco-Arabists have edited and published many manuscripts, which they have compared with the original Greek sources. This work produced significant results, which served as the main source in my investigation. Third, I was able to collect some manuscripts and their English translations and analyze them myself.

My purpose is straightforward: to (a) describe the history of the practice of Arabic translation, (b) redefine translation studies to encompass the history of Arabic translation practice, and (c) identify the knowledge sets and skills that translators needed to acquire in the Middle Ages and compare them with the knowledge sets and skills required in other periods of time. The results of such research can be expected to advance translation studies in various ways.

To begin with, taking the Arab world and Arabic as its points of departure, part of the significance of the study is that it discusses translation in areas whose contributions to translation studies have not been large. Many scholars have recently proposed that translation be studied in different parts of the world to establish translation theory on more comprehensive and solid grounds and to limit ethnocentrism in translation studies.[6] Indeed, as Luc van Doorslaer says, "translation studies can only be strengthened if there is more discourse from and about China, other east Asian nations, southeast Asia, India, Turkic cultures, the Arab world, and so forth."[7] In his article "Continentalism and the Invention of Tradition in Translation Studies," Dirk Delabastita raises a very legitimate question: "To what extent are the well-known translation models – say, those discussed in Anthony Pym's Exploring Translation Theories (2010) – tailored to fit translational practices existing in the West only? To what extent is there an ethnocentrism at work in them which can be contested by considering the

[6] Luc van Doorslaer. "(More Than) American Prisms on Eurocentrisms: An Interview Article." In *Eurocentrism in Translation Studies*, edited by Luc van Doorslaer and Peter Flynn (Amsterdam: John Benjamins, 2013), p. 120. Dirk Delabastita. "Continentalism and the Invention of Traditions in Translation Studies." In *Eurocentrism in Translation Studies*, edited by Luc van Doorslaer and Peter Flynn (Amsterdam: John Benjamins, 2013), pp. 30–1.

[7] van Doorslaer, "(More Than) American Prisms on Eurocentrisms," p. 120.

practices and theories from different parts of the world?"[8] To these suggestions, I add that studying translation in different periods of time can also be a good test for our contemporary translation theory and practice. Although the history of translation in different parts of the world has recently been the center of attention for some scholars, there is still much to be done. Examples include Jean Delisle and Judith Woodsworth, who review, in their book *Translators through History*,[9] the history of translation in different parts of the world focusing on the agent, translators themselves, rather than the product of the process.[10] In his book, *Translation and Identity in the Americas*, Edwin Gentzler describes an emerging American theory of translation that, according to Delabastita, "allows for creativity, freedom and change, and has a living relationship with translation practice. It asserts itself against traditional translation theory, which is essentially European, preoccupied with national languages and national literary canons, and entertaining naïve ideas about universality and the reproductivity of identical meanings."[11]

Further, translation theory suffers from a disproportion between studies of literary translation, on the one hand, and scientific translation, on the other hand. Even though there has recently been more attention paid to scientific translation, translation theory is still largely dominated by discussions of literary and religious texts.[12] This study focuses mainly on Arabic translation of science in the Middle Ages and the early nineteenth century. Scientific translation, as described in this study, is substantially different from contemporary translation theory and practice, since translation was not simply a means of communicating meaning but was also a tool of knowledge production.

Besides, Graeco-Arabic translation is a special case that requires new models of translation to account for its unique challenges, whether in the past in the way that translators performed their work or in the present in the designs that researchers use to study these translations. As far as the process of translation is concerned, a major problem that translators faced during the Graeco-Arabic translation movement was the scarcity of manuscripts. More often than not,

---

8 Delabastita, "Continentalism and the Invention of Traditions in Translation Studies," pp. 30–31.

9 Jean Delisle and Judith Woodsworth. *Translators through History* (Amsterdam: John Benjamins, 1995).

10 Delabastita, Dirk (2011) "Continentalism and the Invention of Traditions in Translation Studies". In *Eurocentrism in Translation Studies*, edited by Luc van Doorslaer and Peter Flynn. Special Issue of *Translation and Interpreting Studies* 6(2) 142–156.

11 Delabastita, "Continentalism and the Invention of Traditions in Translation Studies," p. 37. Edwin Gentzler. *Translation and Identity in the Americas: New Directions in Translation Theory* (London: Routledge, 2008).

12 See, for example, the special issue of *The Translator*, "Science in Translation," 2011. See also Maeve Olohan. *Scientific and Technical Translation* (London: Routledge, 2015). Sue Ellen Wright and Leland D. Wright, Jr., eds. *Scientific and Technical Translation* (Amsterdam: John Benjamins, 1993).

translators worked from a single manuscript that may have been damaged and they needed to travel long distances from one learning center to another to obtain a certain manuscript. The translators were committed, under these working conditions, to engaging critically with their source texts, correcting them and filling their gaps. Even when translators had several manuscripts at their disposal, they had to do additional manuscript work, collating a single manuscript or selecting one variant and including all of the others in the margin or interlineally. That process of selecting a variant was not random and required a great deal of background knowledge and critical thinking.

These finished products then went through a long journey of hand copying, copy editing, and revisions before they reached us. In these cases, a translation is defined as a manuscript that is known as a translation and encompasses the original work of the translator as well as the work of subsequent revisers and editors. The long process of hand copying, in addition to rigorous revisions of translations, requires extra caution from the researcher when examining translation strategies. In addition, data on the original translator and the list of editors and revisers are always unavailable or, at best, doubtful, which is an obstacle for studying a certain translator or a certain period of time. That is why the *Risāla Ḥunayn ibn Isḥāq* is substantial for the history of Arabic translation.[13] It informs us about the translations produced by Ḥunayn, as well as the original translators of some texts that Ḥunayn later revised. It also enlightens us on the practice of translation at that time. For example, it makes us aware that the revision of old translations was a common practice and highlights the difficulty of assigning a translation to a certain translator. Although this was an obstacle for medieval Arabic translation research, it does not pose a serious problem for this study, since it examines the common characteristics of Arabic translation, regardless of the identity of the translator or the period of time.

In addition to a lack of secure data and continuous corruption of manuscripts, many source texts are no longer extant today, which hinders the comparison between source and target texts, particularly those translated out of intermediary Syriac. Further, many of the manuscripts that are extant today are still unedited, and much evidence is still buried in them. In spite of that, the available manuscripts are enough to demonstrate a unique translation practice that, unless clouded by our understanding of translation theory today, yields a rich source for understanding the process of translation and its impact on culture.

[13] Ḥunayn ibn Isḥāq. *Risālat Ḥunayn ibn Isḥāq* (Iran: Muṭalaʿāte Islāmi, 1949).

2 The Graeco-Arabic Translation Movement: Historical Background

Although the phrase "the Graeco-Arabic translation movement" is usually used to refer to the translation activities during the Abbasid Caliphate, its early signs and roots can be traced back to the Umayyad period. During the reign of the Umayyads (661–750 CE),[14] Muslim rule expanded over vast areas and the Muslim Empire became one of the largest in history. At their peak, the Umayyads ruled the Middle East, North Africa, the Iberian Peninsula, Persia, and Central Asia. Despite that power, the Umayyads' rule was short lived, spanning a period of only ninety years. The decline began with the military defeat by the Byzantine Empire in 717 CE, and it continued throughout the later Marwanid period (720–50 CE). During that period, dissatisfaction with the Umayyads grew, revolts against them increased, and the Hāshimayya, a movement that denied the legitimacy of Umayyad rule, gained more supporters. Eventually, the weaknesses of the Umayyads encouraged the Abbasids to declare a revolt in 747 CE. Supported by the Persians, Iraqis, and Shiʿites, the Abbasids won a victory against the Umayyads in the Battle of the Great Zab River in 750 CE and put an end to the Umayyad Dynasty.

Nevertheless, the Umayyad Dynasty enjoyed many years of luxury and prosperity, and it was not unlikely that some Umayyad figures such as Khālid ibn Yazīd (668–704 CE) or ʿUmar ibn Abd al-ʿAzīz (682–720 CE) commissioned some scientific translations into Arabic. Khālid ibn Yazīd was the son of the second Umayyad caliph, Yazīd I, and brother of the third caliph, Muʿāwiyya II. He was supposed to succeed Maʿāwiyya II, but the throne was taken over by his second cousin, Marwan ibn al-Ḥakam. As a result, it was said that Khālid turned his attention to science. In his book *Al-Fahrist*, Ibn al-Nadīm mentions that Khālid ibn Yazīd ibn Muʿāwiyya, who loved science and paid great attention to medicine, commissioned some Greek physicians who used to visit Egypt and who were good at Arabic to translate books from Greek into Arabic.[15] Even though these reports were contested,[16] they indicate that scientific translation was not totally extrinsic to the Umayyad culture. According to Franz Rosenthal, "practical usefulness" was the purpose of translation in the Umayyad period.[17] The Arabs needed information, whether medical, chemical, or even philosophical, and they were happy to get that

[14] The Umayyad Dynasty was divided between two branches of the family: the Sufyānids (reigned from 661 to 684 CE), who were descendants of Muʿāwiyya ibn Abī Sufyān, and the Marwanids (reigned from 684 to 750 CE), that is, Marwān I ibn al-Ḥakam and his successors.

[15] Ibn Al-Nadīm. *Al-Fahrist* (Beirut: Dār al-Miʿrifa, n.d.), p. 338.

[16] See, for example, Dimitri Gutas. *Greek Thought, Arabic Culture: The Graeco-Arabic Translation Movement in Baghdad and Early ʿAbbāsid Society (2nd–4th/8th–10th Centuries)* (New York: Routledge, 1998), p. 24.

[17] Franz Rosenthal. *The Classical Heritage in Islam Arabic Thought and Culture* (London: Routledge, 2005).

information from an Arabic translator or directly from a Greek scholar. Although these activities were individual projects, they indicated a rich intellectual life and a good foundation for the Abbasid translation movement.

Another significant event that took place during the Umayyad Dynasty and paved the way for the Abbasid translation movement was the translation of the *dīwān* (administrative apparatus) into Arabic. The *dīwān* was not simply an official record of salaries, lands, and taxes; it included far more complex operations. As George Saliba convincingly argues,

> Was it not part of the duties of the administrator of the public treasury (*bayt al-māl*) to see to it that the right proportion of gold is cast in the minted dinars, together with what all that implies by way of managing alloys, composition of metals, and exacting weights and measures? Wouldn't such functions include some alchemy, or at least overlap with it, or what was then called *al-ṣan'a*, that was being sought by Khalid? Wasn't this *ṣan'a* also connected to pharmaceutical sciences, and the knowledge of weights and measures, as well as others?[18]

Although we do not have the manuals translated for administrative purposes, it is reasonable to say that the translation of the *dīwān* required a high-level effort to translate scientific works and train new staff.

Further, although the number of works translated during the Umayyad period was few, they were significant, since they set the framework for later work. The early translations from Syriac and Pahlavi introduced the Arabic translators to the techniques of translation and laid the foundation for critical and creative engagement with the source texts.[19] There are then two immediate traditions that we need to examine in order to understand medieval Arabic translation.

To begin with, the Syriac tradition of scientific translation provides a good source for understanding the practice of Arabic translation. During the fifth and sixth centuries, translation activities moved eastward into Persia (Syria and Iraq). This resulted in waves of immigrations of Christian dissidents who suffered ill treatment under the Orthodox Byzantine Church. Under prejudice against pro-Nestorian, and to a lesser degree pro-Monophysite, teachings, teachers and intellectuals of these communities had to immigrate to Persia and rebuild their schools, where they resumed their intellectual activities of studying, commenting on, and translating the Hellenistic knowledge. These new learning centers, an example of which was Jundīshapūr, were a melting pot for two traditions: the

---

18 George Saliba. *Islamic Science and the Making of the European Renaissance* (Cambridge, MA: MIT Press, 2007), p. 57.

19 What Mona Baker says in general terms, namely that "the Persians in particular were instrumental in shaping the intellectual development of Muslim society," applies very well to the Arabic translation tradition, as we will see shortly (Mona Baker. "Arabic Tradition." In *Routledge Encyclopedia of Translation Studies*, edited by Mona Baker (London: Routledge, 2001), p. 319).

Roman and the Perso-Indian traditions.[20] These Syriac translators brought with them the long tradition of Roman translation, but, in their new context, they were able to substantially develop it, whether with the quantity or content of translation. Therefore, beginning from the early fifth century, the focus of translation was no longer the Bible and patristic texts as a larger number of secular texts began to be included. By the seventh century, a significant amount of Greek science and philosophy was being translated into Syriac.[21] These translations were totally different from the Roman appropriation of Greek knowledge, as they were literal renditions. As a result, many new Greekisms – loan words as well as syntactic structures – were introduced into Syriac.

This Syriac translation movement was significant for the Arabic translators because it provided "the stimuli for an increased awareness of technique and the honing of translation skills. Indeed, in more than one instance, the work of these earlier translators was used as a focal point for debate on the best methods to render Greek works into Arabic."[22] One example is how Sergius of Reshʿayna was said to describe his translation approach: "I have taken great care to remain entirely faithful to what I found in the manuscript, neither adding anything to what the philosopher wrote nor leaving anything out."[23] Although Sergius claimed that his method of translation was word for word, modern criticism confirms that his translations were a mixture of literal and free rendering, the very method that is attested to by analyzing Arabic translations, even though Arabic translators also made claims similar to those of Sergius.

The Perso-Indian tradition of scientific translation is another important source for understanding the Arabic approach to translation.[24] Scott Montgomery gives the example of the "zīj" text as a representation of the practice of Pahlavi translation and concludes the following:

> This type of tracing of sources and influences suggests several important conclusions. First, no individual work was viewed as sacred during this period, to be left unmodified. If there were sages of astronomy, prophets and magi from the past whose fame was unalterable, such was far from the case with regard to their actual writings. Pieces of various texts, phrases, words, titles, tables, calculations, and so forth might all be combined and recombined to produce a needed manuscript. Frequently, this involved the updating of older tables and retranslation of accompanying text, but it included many other aspects as well, such as the rearrangement and editing of one work and its insertion into another. Second, the great Ptolemy, whose

[20] Syed Nomanul Haq. "The Indian and Persian Background." In *History of Islamic Philosophy*, edited by Seyyed Hossein Nasr and Oliver Leaman (London: Routledge, 1996), p. 128.
[21] Montgomery, *Science in Translation.* [22] Montgomery, *Science in Translation*, p. 71.
[23] Montgomery, *Science in Translation*, p. 73.
[24] See Haq, "The Indian and Persian Background."

> *Syntaxis* had surely achieved no small degree of fame by this time, was also seen as simply one more useful source, though an important one. Indeed, Ptolemy could even be found wanting in certain comparative respects and subjected to redaction. Third, the city of Jundishapur, with its cosmopolitan institutions of learning, acted as a type of marketplace for textual goods. These products were constantly being transferred, adapted to current uses, and sent on their way again. There appears to have been, if not exactly a constant search, at least a standing interest in news of any overlooked or newly produced work that might aid in a particular purpose.[25]

To sum up, the Arabic translation movement combined features from the Roman, Syriac, and the Pahlavi translation traditions. Like the Romans, they respected the Greek philosophers, scientists, and astronomers and looked to them as models to imitate, thus restricting their originality to epitomes and commentaries on these works. However, they did not displace the Greek texts. Like the Syriac translators, they acknowledged the Greek authors and texts, and mixed word-for-word and sense-for-sense approaches to make their texts accessible to a wider readership. Finally, like the Pahlavi translators, they did not look at the Greek texts as sacred texts; hence, they engaged critically and creatively with them, correcting, reordering, and adding new thought to them.

These features are present in the practice of early translators such as Māsarjawayh. Māsarjawayh, known as the physician of Baṣra, where he lived, was a Jewish physician and translator. He translated the medical *Pandects* of the archdeacon or presbyter Aaron of Alexandria (c. 610–41 CE) from Syriac into Arabic. This translation, which consisted of thirty chapters – to which Māsarjawayh added two chapters of his own – might be the first scientific translation into Arabic. This translation was preserved in the library of the court until Caliph ʿUmar ibn ʿAbd al-ʿAzīz put it to the use of Muslim scholars. Māsarjawayh also authored a few treatises in Arabic including "The Virtues of Foods: Their Advantage and Their Disadvantage" and "The Virtues of Medical Plants: Their Advantage and Their Disadvantage." Neither the translations nor the treatises were preserved, and they were known only by references in other writings.[26]

Another important early translator of the Umayyad period, whose translations assist in understanding the Arabic translation practice in general, is ʿAbd Allah ibn al-Muqaffaʿ (d. 759/60 CE). One of Ibn al-Muqaffaʿ's major contributions is the use of literature to advise kings and princes in what is known as

[25] Montgomery, *Science in Translation*, p. 81.

[26] Aḥmad Ibn Abī Uṣaybiʿa. *Uyūn Al-anbā' Fī Ṭabaqāt Al-aṭibbā'* (Cairo: Al-Wahbiyya, 1882), pp. 232–4. Richard Gottheil and Max Schloessinger. "Masarjawaih or Masarjoyah or Masarjis." In *Jewish Encyclopedia*. www.jewishencyclopedia.com/articles/10458-masarjawaih.

the literary genre of “mirrors for princes.” He also served as a *kātib* (chancery secretary) in the Umayyad Caliphate before its fall, which gave him experience in the affairs of the state, which, in turn, helped him to perfect the political writings of his time. He is well-known, however, for his translation of *Kalīla wa-Dimna* from Pahlavi into Arabic.

3 The Golden Age of the Abbasids

The Abbasids took their name from the Prophet Muhammad's uncle ʿAbbās ibn Abd al-Muṭṭalib (566–653 CE), from whom they descended. They were able to sustain their caliphate from 750 to 1517 CE, although from 861 CE, they began losing different areas of their empire to autonomous dynasties. The first Abbasid caliph was Abu al-Abbās al-Saffāḥ (722–54 CE). The title "al-Saffāḥ" refers to the blood shedding undertaken under his leadership to eliminate the Umayyads. Al-Saffāḥ was succeeded by Abū Jaʿfar al-Manṣūr (714–75 CE), who was the first Abbasid caliph to sponsor the translation movement.

Under al-Manṣūr's leadership, many prominent translators flourished. Abū Yaḥya ibn al-Baṭrīq (730–815 CE), a Syrian scholar and translator, was the official translator of al-Manṣūr. He translated some medical works of Galen and Hippocrates from Greek into Arabic. He also translated Ptolemy's *Tetrabiblos* (*Kitāb al-Samāʾ*) and Aristotle's *Meteorology* (*Kitāb al-Āthār al-ʿUlwiyah*). When al-Manṣūr sent emissaries to the Byzantine emperor in Constantinople requesting manuscripts, the emperor sent some manuscripts, including Euclid's most famous work, *Elements*, which was translated by ibn al-Baṭrīq.[27]

Another famous Greek-into-Arabic translator in the court of al-Manṣūr was Jūrjis ibn Jibrīl (d. 771 CE), who came to the court to treat the caliph and, having succeeded in his mission, he and his pupils after him were hired as court physicians. According to the report, al-Manṣūr had an upset stomach in the year he built Baghdad, and the more his physicians treated him, the worse he felt. Finally, he consulted with his physicians, who all agreed that Jūrjis ibn Jibrīl, at that time the head physician in Jundayshāpūr, the intellectual center of the Sassanid Empire and home to a teaching hospital, was the most acknowledged physician. Listening to the caliph and examining his condition, Jūrjis successfully treated al-Manṣūr, who was soon his old self again. This action gained Jūrjis the favor of the caliph. Jūrjis continued to serve al-Manṣūr until 768 CE, when Jūrjis fell seriously ill and asked the caliph for permission to go back to Jundayshāpūr. Later, al-Manṣūr asked Jūrjis to come back to Baghdad, but Jūrjis was not well and sent one of his students to the court. Other members of the Bakhtishūʿ family of physicians included Jūrjis' son, Bakhtishūʿ, who was no less skillful than his father and who served as the personal physician of Hārūn al-Rashīd. The grandson of Jūrjis, Jibrīl ibn Bakhtishūʿ (d. 824/5 CE), was also a physician, and he was the personal physician of Hārūn al-Rashīd and al-Maʾmūn. Among the eminent pupils of Jibrīl ibn Bakhtishūʿ was Yūḥannā ibn

[27] Imad Al Din M. N. Al-Jubouri. *History of Islamic Philosophy: With View of Greek Philosophy and Early History of Islam* (Hertford: Bright Pen, 2004), pp. 189–90.

Masawayh (777–857 CE), a physician from Jundayshāpūr who translated medical works from Greek into Syriac.

Al-Manṣūr was succeeded by his son Abū ʿAbd Allah Muhammad (745–85 CE), and since it had become the tradition of the Abbasid caliphs to take exalted titles that gave them divine authority, al-Manṣūr – himself having a title that implied divine victory and assistance – gave his son the title "al-Mahdi," that is, "the one guided by God." It was a prominent name because, according to Sunni Muslims, it refers to the eschatological figure who would save the world at the end of times. Al-Mahdi, who reigned from 775 CE to his death in 785 CE, was succeeded by al-Hādi, who in turn was succeeded by his son, Hārūn al-Rashīd (766–809 CE). Hārūn al-Rashīd decided to divide the empire, upon his death, between his two sons, al-Amīn and al-Maʾmūn, whose titles meant "the trustworthy" and "the trusted one," respectively. That division resulted in a civil war that lasted for over two years (811–13 CE) and ended with the victory of al-Maʾmūn, who reigned from 813 CE to his death in 833 CE.

Among the well-known translators in the courts of Hārūn al-Rashīd and al-Maʾmūn were al-Ḥajjāj ibn Yūsuf ibn Maṭar (786–833 CE), Ḥunayn ibn Isḥāq (809–73 CE), and his son Isḥāq (830–910 CE). Ibn Maṭar was a mathematician and translator. He produced two translations of Euclid's *Elements*. The first, apparently based upon one manuscript, was translated in the early ninth century for Yaḥyā ibn Khālid (d. 805 CE), the vizier of Caliph Hārūn al-Rashīd. In the 820s CE, Ḥajjāj produced his second revised translation for Caliph al-Maʾmūn. Ḥajjāj also translated Ptolemy's *Almagest*. Two versions of that translation are extant today. One of these two translations is complete, whereas the second only contains Books I–IV.

Ḥunayn ibn Isḥāq and his son Isḥāq were among the most influential translators and scientists in the Graeco-Arabic translation movement. Ḥunayn ibn Isḥāq was born in the ancient city of al-Ḥīra (south of present-day Kufa in Iraq). He traveled to Baghdad to seek a career in medicine. In Baghdad, he studied under Yūḥannā ibn Māsawayh, the court physician at the time. It seemed that Ḥunayn was too curious, and he asked many questions. His teacher, already short tempered, was disappointed, particularly in the fact that Ḥunayn was from ʿIbād of Ḥīra, whose members were mostly merchants making a living from exchanging money. The teacher, not unlike most of the physicians of Jundīshāpūr, was unsympathetic toward the people of Ḥīra, and he was not willing to teach his profession to the merchants' sons. Thus, one day when Ḥunayn asked his teacher to clarify a point, the teacher was so upset that he dismissed Ḥunayn from his classes, reprimanding him and advising him to work as a merchant like his people instead of learning medicine. The humiliation was so immense that Ḥunayn left the class crying and disappeared for almost two years.[28]

Ḥunayn did not give up the study of medicine but turned his attention to the study of Greek for a while. At that time, the Abbasid caliph, al-Maʾmūn, had at his disposal medical Greek manuscripts that the court physician, Jibrīl ibn Bakhtishūʿ, commissioned Ḥunayn to translate. That was the beginning of a glorious career for Ḥunayn. He became the most productive translator in the translation movement and authored important medical works in Arabic. He was also the teacher of important translators in the movement such as Ḥubaysh ibn al-Ḥasan (c. the second half of the ninth century).

After al-Maʾmūn, the translation movement continued to flourish, and Baghdad continued to attract prominent translators and scholars. Examples include Qusṭā ibn Lūqa (830/40–912/22 CE) and Thābit ibn Qurra (826/36–901 CE). Qusṭā ibn Lūqā was born in the city of Baʿalbak (present-day Lebanon) and moved to Baghdad, probably during the reign of al-Mutawakkil, who reigned from 847 to 861 CE. Lūqā, of Greek Christian origin, was a physician, philosopher, mathematician, and translator. He knew Greek, Syriac, and Arabic, and he translated, revised, and wrote treatises on mathematics, medicine, astronomy, and philosophy.[29] He was among the most prominent figures in the Graeco-Arabic translation movement, whose authority in medicine, according to Ibn al-Nadīm, surpassed that of Ḥunayn ibn Isḥāq.[30]

Thābit ibn Qurra was known as al-Ṣābiʾ Thābit ibn Qurra Al-Ḥarrānī, where "al-Ṣābiʾ" refers to his religion as a worshiper of the stars, and Ḥarrān (in present-day Turkey) refers to the city where he was born and grew up. As a member of the Sabians, who were a Hellenized Semitic astral cult and worshipers of stars, Thābit ibn Qurra mastered astronomy and astrology. He moved to Baghdad as a young man, on the suggestion of Muḥammad ibn Mūsa ibn Shākir, who was impressed by Thābit ibn Qurra's knowledge of Syriac, Greek, and Arabic. In Baghdad, he received training in mathematics and medicine. He returned to Ḥarrān where he was accused of heresy and was forced to escape back to Baghdad. He was appointed the court astronomer for Caliph al-Muʿtaḍid (reigned 892–902 CE). He became one of the most

[28] Ibn Abī Uṣaybiʿa, *Uyūn Al-anbā' Fī Ṭabaqāt Al-aṭibbā'*, pp. 1, 185.

[29] The following are among the best-known astronomical works by Qusṭā ibn Lūqā: *Kitāb fī al-cAmal bi al-Kurra al-Nujūmiyya* (On the Use of the Celestial Globe), *Ḥayʾāt al-aflāk* (On the Configuration of Celestial Bodies), *Kitāb al-Madkhal ilā ʿIlm al-Nujūm* (Introduction to the Science of Astronomy – Astrology), *Kitāb al-Madkhal ilā al-Hayʾa wa-Ḥarakāt al-Aflāk wa-ʾl-Kawākib* (Introduction to the Configuration and Movements of Celestial Bodies and Stars), *Kitāb fī al-cAmal bi al-Asṭurlāb al-Kurrī* (On the Use of the Spherical Astrolabe), and *Kitāb fī al-cAmal bi al-Kurra Dhāt al-Kursī* (On the Use of the Mounted Celestial Sphere).

[30] Al-Nadīm, *Al-Fahrist*, p. 410.

influential mathematicians, physicians, astronomers, and translators in the Abbasid period. His translations include works by the Greek mathematicians Euclid, Archimedes, Apollonius of Perga, and Ptolemy. He revised Ḥunayn ibn Isḥāq's translation of Euclid's *Elements*. He was also the author of important treatises on mathematics and astronomy. By the time of Thābit ibn Qurra and his fellow translators, the Arabization of Greek knowledge had reached a peak. Like the circles of Ḥunayn ibn Isḥāq and al-Kindī, Thābit contributed a great many neologisms to the Arabic language, which facilitated the comprehension and utilization of science and, eventually, of original Arabic science.[31]

It is common to divide the Abbasid Caliphate into three overlapping periods as far as translation is concerned:[32]

- The first period is 753–809 CE, the time of the two caliphs Abū Jaʿfar al-Manṣūr and Hārūn al-Rashīd. During that period, al-Manṣūr established Baghdad (in 762 CE), and Hārūn al-Rashīd was said to establish the *bayt al-ḥikma* (house of wisdom) to be a public library after the palace library became too small for the manuscripts collected for the Abbasid court and their translations. With the exception of Ibn al-Muqaffaʿ, the celebrated Persian translator and thinker, the translators from this period are little known. They were mostly from Christian Aramaic clans from southern Iran and Iraq, and their translations were mostly of astronomy and astrology. This group of translators is different from the translators of the second and third periods, who were Hellenized.
- The second period covered two centuries and started during the time of ʿAbd Allah al-Maʾmūn. This second period is the golden age of translation, when translation became a state-sponsored activity. It received abundant support, both financially and politically, from the court and the elite. The two major groups of translators, that of al-Kindī and Ḥunayn ibn Isḥāq, operated in that phase. By the end of this period, most of the Hellenistic works had been

[31] Salah Basalamah. "The Notion of Translation in the Arab World: A Critical Developmental Perspective." In *A World Atlas of Translation*, edited by Yves Gambier and Ubaldo Stecconi (Amsterdam: John Benjamins, 2019), pp. 169–92.

[32] See Aḥmad Amīn, *Ḍuḥā al-ʾIslām* (Cairo: Hindawi Foundation for Education and Culture, 2011). See also Muhammad Abdelraouf Awni, *Tārīkh Al-Tarjama Al-ʿArabiyya Bayna Al-Sharq Al-ʿArabi Wa Al-Gharb Al-ʾŪrubi*, 2nd ed. (Cairo: Adāb, 2012), p. 86. Richard Walzer distinguished four consecutive groups of translators within the Graeco-Arabic translation movement. The first group appeared with the beginning of the translation movement until the accession of al-Ma'mūn (ruled 813–33 CE). The second group spanned the reign of al-Ma'mūn and al-Muʿtaṣim from 813 to 842 CE. The third group operated from the reign of al-Muʿtaṣim until the first half of the tenth century. The fourth group continued the work of translation in the tenth and eleventh centuries. Whereas the translators of the first group were unknown, the key figures in the second, third, and fourth groups were al-Kindī, Ḥunayn ibn Isḥāq, and Abū Bishr Mattā, respectively. This is referred to in Vagelpohl, *Aristotle's Rhetoric in the East*, p. 18.

translated, and the standardization of methodology and terminology was achieved.[33]

- The third period started in 912 CE and continued until the fall of the Abbasid and the beginning of the Mamluk Sultanate, and it was generally a downward movement of translation. During that period, there were a few Aristotelian treatises that were never translated into Arabic, such as the *Posterior Analytics* and the *Poetics*, which were taken care of by Abū Bishr Mattā, Yaḥya ibn ʿAdī, ʿIsā ibn Isḥāq ibn Zurʿa, and al-Ḥasan ibn Suwār. The reason why these works were not among the early translations is that these parts were removed by Christian authorities from the curriculum in Alexandria because they were considered harmful to Christianity. This restriction was lifted after the Muslim conquest. It is the generation of Abū Bishr Mattā that was credited with introducing these parts of the *Organon* to the Arabic culture.[34]

Therefore, there is no need, for the purpose of this study, to describe the political situation of the Abbasids beyond al-Maʾmūn, since it was around that time that the Abbasids enjoyed the peak of their golden age and during which translation reached its peak. It was a period of peace and prosperity during which the arts, poetry, science, translation, and learning in general were generously sponsored by the caliphs.

In contrast with the Umayyads, who annexed vast areas to the emerging Muslim empire, the Abbasids focused primarily on internal affairs. Among the significant characteristics of the Abbasid reign was the inclusion of non-Arabs in the community. They relied on the Persians (particularly the Barmakids) in administration, and they adopted many of their etiquettes. The combined accomplishments of the Umayyads and the Abbasids (i.e. the expansion of the Muslim empire over vast areas and the acceptance of multicultural and multilingual norms) were significant for the translation movement for two main reasons.

First, the success of the translation movement relied on men capable of translating from Syriac, Greek, and Persian. Such men existed as part of the Islamic empire after the annexation of huge areas from other empires surrounding Arabia. In addition, the existence of speakers of other languages in the Muslim empire made translation, particularly for business and administrative purposes, a necessity. Further, soon under the Umayyads' reign, Arabic became the state official language of administration, commerce, and learning. Accordingly, those who spoke Arabic among the administrators, merchants,

33 Vagelpohl, *Aristotle's Rhetoric in the East*.

34 Vagelpohl, *Aristotle's Rhetoric in the East*, pp. 57–8.

men of letters, and scientists "found themselves in an advantaged position, not only politically and socially but intellectually."[35] In this sense, the history of Arabic translation had its roots in the Umayyad period. Second, the lifting of the political and religious barriers helped equip the Abbasid court with a great number of scholars who were experts in their fields, as well as multilingual, so they were able to transmit their knowledge and translate key texts in their fields.[36]

The newly founded capital of al-Mansūr, Baghdad, became, together with older cities such as Jundayshāpūr and Ḥarrān, a center of learning. In these learning centers, translations of classical works of medicine, mathematics, astronomy, and natural philosophy flourished. That rise of translation activities was the result of a constellation of circumstances. In his book *Greek Thought, Arabic Culture*, Dimitri Gutas analyzes the Abbasid translation movement as a social phenomenon that was the result of its context. Above all, without the prosperity and luxury of the court and the interest of the caliphs themselves, there was doubt that translation could gain its momentum. Abbasid caliphs such as Hārūn al-Rashīd and al-Maʾmūn showed great interest in making manuscripts available for Arabic translators, and they were ready to endow bags of gold for finished translations. The translators themselves were content to translate for the caliph's gold, but they also had clear research interest in their work.

Sometimes, the individual propensities of the caliph determined the kind of material to translate. For example, al-Ghassānī compiled a book for al-Mahdī on falconry because the caliph (al-Mahdī) liked falconry.[37] Al-Ghassānī not only used Arabic sources but also incorporated foreign sources. That book, which became the archetype of Arabic literature on falconry, was mainly possible because of al-Mahdī, who liked falconry, and because of the translation culture that enabled Ghassānī to include both Arabic and foreign sources, since without that culture, he could have compiled only Arabic sources.

The translation movement was not supported by the court alone; it was supported by the entire elite Abbasid society. The funding was enormous, and it came from both public and private sources. This can be analyzed in light of the Islamic stress on learning (*ʿilm*) as one of the duties of all Muslims.[38] This can

[35] Marshall G. S. Hodgson. *The Venture of Islam, Volume 2: The Expansion of Islam in the Middle Periods* (Chicago: University of Chicago Press, 2009), p. 235.

[36] Gutas, *Greek Thought, Arabic Culture*ʿ, p. 16.

[37] Gutas, *Greek Thought, Arabic Culture*ʿ, p. 74.

[38] One reason suggested by Rosenthal for the success of the translation movement is the emphasis that the Qur'ān places on the role of knowledge and the responsibility of every individual towards knowledge (for example, Qur'ān 20:114, 39:9, and 58:11) (Rosenthal, *The Classical Heritage in Islam Arabic Thought and Culture*). There is also a Hadith that says, "Seek knowledge as far as China." Even though that Hadith might be fabricated, the fact that it became widespread in the medieval Muslim community indicates a prevailing spirit of appreciating

also be analyzed in light of the needs of the Muslim community. Thus, according to Dimitri Gutas, the reasons for the rise of the Abbasid translation movement were different from those for the rise of translation activity of Aristotelian and other ancient texts from Greek and Arabic into Latin in western Europe in the twelfth century. In Europe, the rise of the new class of the bourgeoisie necessitated a new kind of knowledge that was different from the traditional church learning of the clergy. In the Abbasid society, the longevity of the translation movement can partially be explained by considering "the demand for applied knowledge in the rapidly evolving social climate of Baghdad and [of] the demand for theoretical knowledge by the scientific and philosophical tradition in the process of formation."[39]

The movement started with an interest in the applied sciences of astrology, astronomy, and mathematics. This initial interest in the applied sciences eventually created a need for theoretical foundation, so the translation movement was expanded to include philosophical sciences. For example, Aristotle's *Topics* was needed to teach Muslims debate, so they could defend their religion against Christians and Jews, and Aristotle's *Physics* was needed to provide them with factual information to be used in theological debates. Thus, the translated works had the added value of immediate use and applicability, whether it was to medicine, philosophy, or astrology. Similarly, astrological history was translated and adopted to support the Abbasid revolution. Astrological history described cycles of power, such as emergence, dominance, and downfall, as governed by the stars and planets.[40] The cycles of power and the renewal of knowledge were Zoroastrian beliefs. The Muslim translators and scholars Islamized those ideas so that the decrees of the stars were by the command of God, so any resistance to the Abbasid rise would be futile or against the very will of God.

knowledge and learning. Another more authentic Hadith says, "Whoever treads a path in search of knowledge, God makes their path to paradise easier." Some scholars argue that *ʿilm* (learning) is usually used by Muslims to refer to religious and Arabic language sciences, but the fact that the financial support for the translation movement was greater than the financial support for religious scholars and grammarians indicates a wider understanding of knowledge and learning in the Abbāsid period.

39 Gutas, *Greek Thought, Arabic Culture*, p. 104.

40 One of the very first books translated into Arabic was Abū Sahl's *Kitāb al-Nahmuṭān*, whose political purpose, according to Dimitri Gutas, was to confirm that the stars had ordained that it was the time for the Abbasids to rise to power and renew science (Gutas, *Greek Thought, Arabic Culture*, p. 45). See also Al-Nadīm, *Al-Fahrist*, p. 382.

4 Key Characteristics of Arabic Translation in the Medieval Period

As explained above, the early Arabic translations from Pahlavi and Syriac are significant, since they explain key features of the Arabic translation tradition. From the Pahlavi, Arabic translators took the idea that a translator can add new thought to a translation. Thus, when Ibn al-Muqaffaʿ translated *Kalīla wa-Dimna* from intermediary Pahlavi, he was inspired by translators before him who added their own original stories to the translation. From the Syriac, the Arabic translators learned to be mindful of faithfulness to source texts while integrating word-for-word and sense-for-sense approaches to translation and Christianizing their pagan sources. Therefore, before describing in depth the key features of the Arabic translation movement, we will examine a prominent Syriac translator before Islam, namely Sergius of Reshʿaynā (d. 536 CE).

Syriac was the first Semitic language into which Greek philosophy was translated. The key figure in the first significant translations from Greek into Syriac was Sergius of Reshʿaynā, a physician, theologian, and philosopher in the fifth and sixth centuries. Sergius studied in the school of Alexandria and became well known for his Syriac translations in the fields of theology, philosophy, and medicine, particularly the corpus of Pseudo-Dionysius the Areopagite. He also had a grand project in mind, as he expressed his intention to write about all parts of Aristotle's philosophy. The project, however, was too ambitious, and only the first few books of the *Organon* were translated.[41] Sergius' approach to translation is noteworthy, as he reconciled the "pagan" wisdom of the Greeks with Christianity,[42] and he did not introduce Greek philosophy in Syriac as dry texts but as a living system of problems.

Part of the significance of Sergius is that he established a tradition that was followed by other Christian translators and commentators on Aristotle, and he later played a significant role in the rise of Arabic philosophy.[43] The school of Alexandria, where Sergius flourished, rather than any of the intellectual centers that existed at that time, such as Antioch, Edessa, Nisibis, Qenneshrīn, Jundayshāpūr, Marw, and Ḥarrān, was the main place for learning philosophy.[44] Translators in Alexandria did not simply convey the meaning of the Greek texts but engaged critically with them. That pattern was adopted in

[41] Gutas, *Greek Thought, Arabic Culture*ʿ, p. 21.

[42] Emiliano Fiori. "Sergius of Reshʿaynā." In *Encyclopedia of Medieval Philosophy*, edited by Henrik Lagerlund (Dordrecht: Springer Netherlands, 2011), pp. 1185–8.

[43] Cristina D'ancona. "Greek into Arabic: Neoplatonism in Translation." In *The Cambridge Companion to Arabic Philosophy*, edited by Peter Adamson and Richard C. Taylor (Cambridge: Cambridge University Press, 2005), p. 19.

[44] D'ancona, "Greek into Arabic: Neoplatonism in Translation," p. 20.

Baghdad, which became an intellectual center where translation developed into "a systematic assimilation of Greek scientific and philosophical learning."[45]

In two separate chapters in *Interpreting the Bible and Aristotle in Late Antiquity*, Adam McCollum and Emiliano Fiori indicate that Sergius of Reshʿaynā employed two different approaches in his translation of *De Mundo* and Dionysius.[46] In *De Mundo*, he made changes and employed additions to clarify matters for his Syriac readers only when absolutely necessary, deleting at the same time nothing of substance. With Dionysius, Emiliano Fiori calls Sergius' approach "dialectical fidelity," since he practiced control over the text to prevent any of Dionysius' Neoplatonic nuances from creeping into the biblical text. This analysis allows Josef Lössl and John Watt to conclude that "the activity of Sergius thus turns out to be considerably more coherent than might appear at first sight."[47] Consistency of approach becomes clearer when we focus on his purpose rather than his approach to translation. His purpose was to offer his Syriac readers an honest translation of the original text that was as consistent as possible with the Bible because the target text could be true only when it was consistent with the Bible.[48]

This kind of critical engagement with source texts reemerged with the Arabic translators, philosophers, and commentators. Sergius, in Alexandria, broke "from the Plato and Proclus of his pagan masters and linked Aristotle in the program with the Bible and Dionysius."[49] The process was reverted around four centuries later in Baghdad when al-Fārābī (870–950 CE), the renowned early Islamic philosopher, broke from the Bible and Dionysius and reconciled the Greek philosophy with Islam. Averroes, in the twelfth century, as Abid al-Jabri

[45] D'ancona, "Greek into Arabic: Neoplatonism in Translation," p. 21.

[46] Emiliano Fiori. "Sergius of Reshaina and Pseudo-Dionysius: A Dialectical Fidelity." In *Interpreting the Bible and Aristotle in Late Antiquity: The Alexandrian Commentary Tradition Between Rome and Baghdad*, edited by Josef Lössl and John Watt (Farnham, UK: Ashgate, 2011), pp. 180–94. Adam McCollum. "Sergius of Reshaina as Translator: The Case of the De Mundo." In *Interpreting the Bible and Aristotle in Late Antiquity: The Alexandrian Commentary Tradition Between Rome and Baghdad*, edited by Josef Lössl and John Watt (Farnham, UK: Ashgate, 2011), pp. 165–78.

[47] Josef Lössl and John Watt. "Introduction." In *Interpreting the Bible and Aristotle in Late Antiquity: The Alexandrian Commentary Tradition Between Rome and Baghdad*, edited by Josef Lössl and John Watt (Farnham, UK: Ashgate, 2011), pp. 1–10.

[48] Another explanation of Sergius' approaches to translation is offered by Adam McCollum, who looks at Sergius as a transitional figure. The sixth century when Sergius lived was a transition between the fourth and fifth centuries, on the one hand, during which time translation approaches were mostly free, and the seventh century, on the other, during which time translation became more literal (McCollum, "Sergius of Reshaina as Translator").

[49] John Watt. "From Sergius to Mattā: Aristotle and Pseudo-Dionysius in the Syriac Tradition." In *Interpreting the Bible and Aristotle in Late Antiquity: The Alexandrian Commentary Tradition Between Rome and Baghdad*, edited by Josef Lössl and John Watt (Farnham, UK: Ashgate: 2011), p. 257.

explains, purified Plato's *The Republic* from unproven opinions (*aqāwīl ghayr burhāniyya*), so he ignored any reference to Greek mythology. He also did not include the first book and part of the second book because it was a debate without proof. Throughout the book, there were parts that Averroes ignored or rearranged so that the final product was presented in a completely new form. *Jawāmiʿ Siyāsat Aflaṭūn* (the Arabic version of Plato's *The Republic*) was not a mere summary or explanation of Plato's work. It was a text reconstructed, so it was void of any unscientific sayings. While Plato writes about war and its laws, Averroes discusses *jihad* and its ethics in Islam. Another example of critical engagement is how Averroes broke the gender bias against women, stating that they could be philosophers and judges. The idea itself was Plato's, but Averroes did not ignore it like al-Fārābī had. Averroes carried out two complementary processes. First, he familiarized the reader with Plato's ideas and, second, he aimed to contextualize these ideas (*tabīʾa*, to use al-Jabri's term) to fit into the Arabic culture.[50]

What the masters learned from Aristotle was to subject any writing, including Aristotle himself, to a relentless critique. They rejected any authority except the authority of reason. Thus, they distinguished between philosophical and theological discourse, which came to be known as Averroism in the latter half of the thirteenth century. This distinction enabled the break with the clerical commentary tradition (i.e. from exposition to critique and the question form of commentary).[51] The distinction between philosophical and theological discourse can be interesting for translation studies. The translation of theological texts, particularly scriptures, focuses on the linguistic analysis of text, is concerned with philological problem-solving, and is stuck between word-for-word and sense-for-sense approaches. This kind of translation focuses solely on communicating the meaning of the source text. By contrast, the history of translation of science and philosophy attests to translation activities that go beyond the communication of meaning and looks at translation as a creative interaction and critical engagement with the text. In this sense, translation is a means of knowledge production rather than simply a means of communicating meaning. The concept of translation as a unified product that cannot be broken up unless one produces inaccuracies narrows our view of translation, turns it into a mechanical process, prioritizes philology over philosophy, and imprisons the translator's reason behind language. It turns the translator into a conservative clergyman before a sacred text.

---

[50] Muhammad Abed al-Jabri. *Al-Mutaqqafūn fī al-Ḥadāra al-ʿArabīya: Miḥnat Ibn Ḥanbal wa-Nakbat Ibn Rušd* (Beirut: Markaz Dirāsāt al-Wiḥda al-ʿArabīya, 1995), p. 143.

[51] Charles H. Lohr. "The Medieval Interpretation of Aristotle." In *The Cambridge History of Later Medieval Philosophy*, edited by Norman Kretzmann, Anthony Kenny, and Jan Pinborg (Cambridge: Cambridge University Press, 2008), p. 80–99.

Sergius of Reshʿaynā is an interesting example as an early translator from the East for two main reasons. First, Sergius was not a translator by profession. He was a polymath whose knowledge spanned medicine, theology, and philosophy, and translation was part of his scientific project. This also applies to all of the Arabic translators of the medieval East who were philosophers, scientists, and writers. Second, in his translations, Sergius was not simply communicating meaning, but was critically engaging with the source text. By relating Aristotle to the Bible, for instance, Sergius used translation to carry out the social function of "maintaining" the target culture.[52] This use of translation to solve social problems, fill scientific gaps, or maintain target cultures would later dominate the Graeco-Arabic translation movement.[53]

[52] I am adopting Peter Berger's term "world-maintaining force." By modifying the source text, Sergius maintains the superiority of Christianity, rather than threatening it by being faithful to the source text. See Peter L. Berger. *The Sacred Canopy: Elements of a Sociological Theory of Religion* (New York: Open Road Integrated Media, 2011).

[53] However, "the most advanced Syriac scientists of the period just before Islam or in early Islamic times" did not develop the Greek science; instead, they asserted that "whoever wants to verify this or that problem, more accurately, he should seek the more advanced texts" (Saliba, *Islamic Science and the Making of the European Renaissance*, p. 60). Thus, Syriac translation was different from the Arabic translation movement in two respects: Syriac translation remained an elite activity and it did not develop the Greek science.

5 Translation Competence

The previous sections introduced some of the most influential translators, philosophers, and scientists in the Graeco-Arabic translation movement in the Umayyad and Abbasid periods, such as Māsarjawayh, Ibrahim al-Fazārī, Abū Yaḥya ibn al-Baṭrīq, al-Ḥajjāj ibn Yūsuf ibn Maṭar, Ḥunayn ibn Isḥāq, Qusṭā ibn Lūqā, Thābit ibn Qurra, Abū Bishr Mattā, Yaḥya ibn ʿAdī, and ʿIsā ibn Isḥāq ibn Zurʿa. Although this list is by no means complete, it gives us an idea of the nature of translation and the skills of the translators. In the following subsections, I describe what is common among these translators and their approach to translation.

Translation as Research

Historians usually refer to two major circles of translation in Baghdad: the first circle is made up of those translators who were content experts and whose interest in translation was part of their scientific research interest.[54] They employed translation to fill gaps in knowledge or solve current problems. They also perceived learning a foreign language as an instrument for furthering their scientific knowledge. Therefore, language pedagogy consisted of reading and discussing a specialized foreign text, which must have positively affected the translators' reading comprehension and mastery over the content. In addition, many of the translators had shared interests and worked in the same intellectual centers, which helped them reach a critical mass of translators and scientists and of texts translated in a certain field.

The second circle is that of Ḥunayn ibn Isḥāq and, slightly earlier than that, the circle of al-Kindī.[55] The circle of al-Kindī shaped the Arabic reception of Greek philosophy.[56] Among the first texts translated in this circle was an adaptation of selections from Plotinus' *Enneads* and Proclus' *Elements of Theology*. The circle also produced the first Arabic translations of Aristotle's

[54] The translators were, as Myriam Salama-Carr points out, scholars in their own right. See Edwin Gentzler. "Macro- and Micro-Turns in Translation Studies." In *Eurocentrism in Translation Studies*, edited by Luc van Doorslaer and Peter Flynn (Amsterdam: John Benjamins, 2013), p. 14.

[55] Abū Yaʿqūb ibn Isḥāq al-Kindī (c. 801–72 CE) was a polymath who wrote extensively on mathematics, medicine, physics, and astrology, besides numerous philosophical topics, especially psychology. Among his well-known philosophical treatises are *Al-Falsafa al-ʿŪlā fīmā dūn al-Ṭabīʿiyyāt wa-al-Tawḥīd* (known in English as *On First Philosophy*) and *On the Intellect*. Al-Kindī relied heavily on Arabic translations produced in his circle, such as the works of Aristotle, the Neoplatonists, and Greek mathematicians and scientists. Among the famous translators in his circle was ʿAbd al-Masīḥ ibn ʿAbd Allah ibn Nāʿima (c. early ninth century), who translated Aristotle's *Sophistical Refutations* and *Physics* into Arabic.

[56] Peter Adamson. "Al-Kindī and the Reception of Greek Philosophy." In *The Cambridge Companion to Arabic Philosophy*, edited by Peter Adamson and Richard C. Taylor (Cambridge: Cambridge University Press, 2005), p. 32.

Metaphysics and *De Caelo*.[57] The group was credited for the rearrangement of Proclus' *Elements of Theology* and Aristotle's *Exposition of the Pure Good*, with the latter being later translated, in Toledo in the twelfth century, from Arabic into Latin.[58] As Peter Adamson states, "The choice of which texts to translate was guided in part by the philosophical concerns of al-Kindī and his collaborators."[59] This conforms to the common practice of translation at that time when translation was part of the research interest of the translator.[60] Within the circle of al-Kindī, changes in the source text during the translation process were carried out for various purposes. For example, abridgements were produced for lengthy works, and explanations were produced for complicated works. Sometimes, the translator's commentaries provided more information and rendered the original work more comprehensible than it was.[61] More significantly, the translators sometimes rearranged and added their own elaborations to the source text. Examples include Aristotle's *De Anima*, *Theology of Aristotle*, and the *Book on the Pure Good* (known in Latin as the *Liber de Causis*).[62] This approach is significant because it indicates how al-Kindī and his circle viewed translation. Translation, within this approach, was not simply a tool for communicating the source text's meaning, but it was also a cultural tool for knowledge production. It had to respond to the conventions of the target language as much as to the contemporary problems and concerns of the translators and their cultural contexts. This resulted in rearranging and supplementing the source text and creating new philosophical terminology in Arabic, which was eventually furthered in original compositions.[63] This tradition of translating, supplementing, and rearranging was later adopted by the Arabic-into-Latin translators of Toledo.[64]

---

[57] D'ancona, "Greek into Arabic," p. 21. [58] D'ancona, "Greek into Arabic," p. 26.

[59] Adamson, "Al-Kindī and the Reception of Greek Philosophy," p. 32.

[60] Similarly, "the translation of philosophical texts from Greek into Arabic, often through the intermediary of Syriac translations, was functional to the attempt, by philosophers such as Abū Bishr Mattā, al-Fārābī and Yaḥyā ibn ʿAdī, to found an Arabic school of philosophy." Alberto Rigolio. "Aristotle's Poetics in Syriac and in Arabic Translations: Readings of 'Tragedy'." *Khristianskii Vostok*, vol. 6, 2013, p. 147.

[61] According to Franz Rosenthal, "This was the case with Aristotle's *Logic* which was translated literally and is preserved for us in literal form but was by preference studied from commentaries." Rosenthal, *The Classical Heritage in Islam Arabic Thought and Culture*, p. 10.

[62] Adamson, "Al-Kindī and the Reception of Greek Philosophy," p. 33.

[63] Peter Adamson concludes that "While it is thus impossible to appreciate al-Kindī's works without knowledge of the Greek tradition, it would be incorrect to say that the only interest of his works is his reception and modification of Greek thought. As indicated above, al-Kindī tries to present Greek philosophy as capable of solving problems of his own time, including problems prompted by Islamic theological concerns." (Adamson, "Al-Kindī and the Reception of Greek Philosophy," p. 46.)

[64] As Charles Burnett states, "The translators from Gerard of Cremona, through Alfred of Shareshill, to Michael Scot and Hermann the German, had filled in the gaps in knowledge among the Latins and, through their translation and interpretation, had recovered the ancient and

The school of Ḥunayn ibn Isḥāq and his son Isḥāq – known for producing many high-quality translations of Aristotle and Galen – was the more important center of translation. Of particular importance to Ḥunayn ibn Isḥāq himself were the medical texts of Galen, which constituted the basis for Ḥunayn's own treatises on medicine, particularly his major contribution to medieval medicine, the Isagoge. As Edward Grant describes it,

> But from our perspective we can see that the Arabic origins of this restitution of Aristotle had a decisive effect on the nature of the medieval curriculum in philosophy. Greek manuscripts provided the raw texts of Aristotle's works. But the Arabic tradition supplied not the "pure" Aristotle of the fourth century BCE, but rather . . . the late Neoplatonic curriculum, in which Aristotle's metaphysics was crowned with a rational theology issuing from the Platonic tradition. Hence the De Causis could naturally be incorporated into a corpus of Aristotle's works. These Neoplatonic elements can be seen even more clearly in other texts of Arabic philosophy which were never integrated into the Aristotelian corpus.[65]

The Isagoge, written by Ḥunayn as an introduction to Galenic medicine, was available in the West quite early, toward the end of the eleventh century; it was the only systematic exposition of medical theory known in this period before the translation of the bulk of the Graeco-Arabic medical corpus. Its conciseness kept it in use as a standard text for over two hundred years, long after European physicians had attained a vastly more detailed knowledge of Galenic theory.[66] The Arabic translation of Galen's commentary on the *Epidemics* is one of the major contributions of Ḥunayn ibn Isḥāq. Its influence on the development of Arabic medicine is well established. Within four hundred years of the production of the translation, no fewer than fifteen medical Arabic authors used the *Epidemics*.[67] For example, both Ḥunayn's translation and summaries are important sources for Abū Bakr Muhammad ibn Zakariyya al-Rāzī (d. 925 CE), who is well known for his medical encyclopedic book, *al-Ḥāwī*. The well-known physician Ibn al-Nafīs (d. 1288 CE), who authored many commentaries on Hippocratic and other medical writings, relied on Ḥunayn's translation of Galen's commentaries on Hippocrates. Other physicians, such as Isḥāq ibn ʿAlī

perennial wisdom." (Charles Burnett. "Arabic into Latin: The Reception of Arabic Philosophy into Western Europe." In *The Cambridge Companion to Arabic Philosophy*, edited by Peter Adamson and Richard C. Taylor (Cambridge: Cambridge University Press, 2005), pp. 375–6.)

[65] Edward Grant. *A Source Book in Medieval Science* (Cambridge, MA:Harvard University Press, 1974).

[66] Grant, *A Source Book in Medieval Science*, p. 705, Note 1.

[67] Bink Hallum. "The Arabic Reception of Galen's *Commentary on Hippocrates' 'Epidemics'*." In *Epidemics in Context: Greek Commentaries on Hippocrates in the Arabic Tradition*, edited by Peter E. Pormann (Berlin: De Gruyter, 2012), p. 185.

al-Ruhāwī (c. 870 CE), Yaʿqūb al-Kasharī (c. 920 CE), Abū al-Ḥasan ʿAlī ibn Riḍwān (d. 1068 CE), and Abū ʿImran Mūsā ibn ʿUbayd Allah ibn Maymūn (Maimonides) (d. 1204 CE) make use of Ḥunayn's works.[68]

Ḥunayn's approach to translation was sometimes dependent on the availability of manuscripts. As Ḥunayn states in his *Risāla*, he traveled to several intellectual centers in search of manuscripts because a single manuscript was not usually enough for a good translation, particularly if it was damaged. For example, when he was twenty years old, he translated Galen's *De Sectis* from a single, and unfortunately damaged, manuscript. However, at the age of forty, he was able to collate a few manuscripts for the same text and produce a better translation.[69] This means that the approach to translation was sometimes affected by the nature of the manuscripts available. By and large, the translations of the school of Ḥunayn and his son Isḥāq were, as Richard Walzer confirms, "extremely good." They were so good that they could help "ascertain the exact meaning of Greek words in the ninth century."[70]

Nevertheless, Ḥunayn's translation of Galen's commentary on Hippocrates is unique for a number of reasons. First, the *Risāla* of Ḥunayn provides us with an adequate amount of information on this text. Ḥunayn tells us that Books 1 and 6 are translated from Greek into Syriac by Ayyūb al-Ruhāwī. Ḥunayn then rendered these Syriac translations into Arabic. As for Book 2, Ḥunayn has a number of manuscripts, out of which he collates one manuscript, translating it into Syriac and then into Arabic. Second, Ḥunayn's Arabic translation of this work proves priceless in the reconstruction of the Greek text, as I will soon explain. More importantly, since the data on the translator of this text are relatively secure, they can provide a good basis for the stylistic features of the translator.[71]

An analysis of Ḥunayn's medical translations indicates that Ḥunayn prioritizes ideas and concepts over linguistic form and clarity over philological accuracy. Although he does not try to achieve one at the expense of the other, he uses strategies that ensure clarity and completeness of ideas more than anything else. Such an attitude is apparent not only from his translation techniques but also from his notes, as well as his *Risāla*. For example, at least twice

68 Uwe Vagelpohl. *Galeni In Hippocratis Epidemiarum Librum I Commentariorum I–III Versionem Arabicam/Galen. Commentary on Hippocrates' Epidemics Book I: Edidit, in Linguam Anglicam Vertit, Commentatus Est* (Berlin: De Gruyter, 2014), pp. 35–47.

69 Isḥāq, *Risālat Ḥunayn ibn Isḥāq*.

70 Richard Walzer. *Greek into Arabic: Essays on Islamic Philosophy* (Cambridge, MA: Harvard University Press, 1962), p. 118.

71 See Uwe Vagelpohl. "Galen, *Epidemics*, Book One: Text, Transmission, Translation." In *Epidemics in Context: Greek Commentaries on Hippocrates in the Arabic Tradition*, edited by Peter E. Pormann (Berlin: De Gruyter, 2012).

in his *Risāla*, he reports that his sponsors are intelligent, experienced, and diligent in studying medicine, which makes him extra careful in conveying the precise meaning of the source text.[72] In addition, when he translates for his own son, he makes sure to write in clear and easy-to-understand language.[73]

An example of how the translators fully engaged scientifically with their translations is what Ḥunayn ibn Isḥāq mentions in his introduction to *Risāla*, that is, that sometimes a translator themselves would commission a retranslation or revision, which means that the translators were fully aware of the significance of each text.[74] Retranslations or revisions of old translations, which were the common practice during the Abbasid translation movement, were also practical solutions, given the significance of each text and the paucity of manuscripts in general. In many cases, they represent a continuous process of scientific engagement with the source text and previous translations.

A good example is found in the life of the Arabic translation of the book of Dioscorides. At the beginning of the book, Abū Dāwūd Sulaymān ibn Ḥassān (944–94 CE), known as Ibn Juljul, a well-known physician of his time and the translator of the book, stated that the first person who translated the book from Greek into Arabic was Iṣṭifan ibn Basīl during the time of the Abbasid Caliph Jaʿfar al-Mutawakkil (822–61 CE). The book was examined by Ḥunayn, who corrected and certified the translation, which was not complete, since Iṣṭifan ibn Basīl translated only those Greek names of drugs that he knew. Other drug names that he did not know, and for which he could not find Arabic equivalents, were left in Greek. He hoped that someone after him would find equivalents in Arabic based on a better knowledge of the drugs.

Two types of engagement are clear here. The first is procedural engagement, as Iṣṭifan ibn Basīl was aware of translation procedures, such as etymological derivation, that can solve the problem of naming. The second is scientific and critical engagement, since he knew that translation was not merely concerned with finding an equivalent, but also with helping the physicians who would read the translation to administer the correct drug. In other words, Iṣṭifan ibn Basīl was concerned not only with making knowledge accessible but also with applying his knowledge. That is, rather than translating science by writing it in another language, he translated science by doing it.

Later, Romanos, the emperor of Constantinople, sent splendid gifts to al-Nāṣir ʿAbd al-Raḥmān ibn Muḥammad, the ruler of Al-Andalus, and those gifts included a copy of the book of Dioscorides. In his letter to al-Nāṣir, Romanos

---

[72] See, for example, Ḥunayn's reference to Muhammad ibn ʿAbd al-Malik al-Wazīr (Isḥāq, *Risālat Ḥunayn ibn Isḥāq*, p. 28) and his reference to Dāwūd, the physician (Isḥāq, *Risālat Ḥunayn ibn Isḥāq*, p. 4).

[73] Isḥāq, *Risālat Ḥunayn ibn Isḥāq*, p. 28.

[74] Isḥāq, *Risālat Ḥunayn ibn Isḥāq*, p. 21.

referred to two major competences of whoever would translate that book. "You will not profit from the book of Dioscorides," wrote Romanos, "unless you have someone with knowledge of the Greek language, who will recognize the characteristics of those drugs."[75] It was clear that knowledge of Ancient Greek (*Yūnānī*), the language of the book, was not enough, and the ability to engage with the book scientifically and critically was equally important.

Romanos sent Niqūlā the monk to explain the book and teach ancient Greek. At that time, there were several physicians who were interested in examining and translating that book. Among those physicians was Ḥasdāy ibn Shaprūṭ al-Isrāʾīlī, who had a good relationship with al-Nāṣir, the ruler of al-Andalus. The monk Niqūlā won the favor of Ibn Shaprūṭ, and they worked together on the Dioscorides project. Ibn Juljul was able to meet both Niqūlā and Shaprūṭ at the time of al-Mustanṣir and learn from them. Soon, however, Niqūlā died, but by the time of his death at the beginning of the reign of al-Mustanṣir al-Ḥakam only a few drugs were not translated, namely the ones that he could not identify. As Ibn Juljul stated,

> I had longed to know the explanation of the *Materia Medica* (*Hayūlā al-ṭibb*), which is the basis for compound drugs, and I had sought it eagerly until God, in His Grace, vouchsafed me this gift, and with the power that He granted to me, I was able to [accomplish] my resolution of reviving what was poorly taught and from which the bodies of the people could not benefit.[76]

This quotation is significant because it shows the nature of translation as a problem-solving activity that is both form- and content-based. The problem was not simply to coin an equivalent to the Greek term, but to use translation as a means of knowledge production that had an impact on people's lives. Thus, translation was soon followed by original composition. Among the books that Ibn Juljul composed were *Kitāb Tafsīr Asmāʾ al-Adwiya al-Mufrada min Kitāb Diyusqūrīdis* (an explanation of the names of the simple drugs in the book of Dioscorides) and *Maqāla fī Dhikr al-Adwiyya allatī Lam Yadhkurhā Diyusqūrīdis fī Kitābih mimmā Yustaʿmal fī Ṣināʿat al-Ṭibb wa-Yuntafaʿ bi-hi wa-Mā Lā Yustaʿmal Likaylā Yughfal Dhikruh* (treaties on the drugs not mentioned by Dioscorides in his book, that is, the profitable drugs used both in medicine and not in medicine, so as not to overlook their mention). These works are a combination of translation and original composition.

75 Uwe Vagelpohl and Ignacio Sanchez. "Why Do We Translate? Arabic Sources on Translation." In *Why Translate Science*, edited by Dimitri Gutas (Leiden: Brill, 2022), pp. 254–376.

76 Aḥmad Ibn Abī Uṣaibiʿa. *A Literary History of Medicine: The 'Uyūn Al-anbāʾ Fī Ṭabaqāt Al-aṭibbāʾ of Ibn Abī Uṣaybiʿah*, translated by Emilie Savage-Smith, Simon Swain, Geert Jan H. van Gelder, I. J. S. Rojo, N. P. Joosse, A. Watson, B. Inksetter, and F. Hilloowala (Leiden: Brill, 2020).

Translation as a Developmental Process

Sometimes, a work by a translator could be of higher quality than their earlier work because it had been produced or revised at a later stage of their life when they had gained more knowledge and experience as a scholar and translator. Modern translation theory explains this improvement as an aspect of the developmental process of translation. For example, the unit of translation – a stretch of source text that a translator can process and transfer to the target language in one attempt – is enlarged when a translator attains higher levels of language proficiency or acquires content schemata, namely a specialist background knowledge in the topic of translation.[77] This explains why the approach of a novice translator is sometimes word for word. Since the unit of translation is a developmental aspect of the translation process, it mainly develops as a result of practice and experience. However, it is also affected by other factors, such as the availability of background knowledge, text type, and text complexity.

For example, commenting on the work of Ḥunayn ibn Isḥāq, Franz Rosenthal remarks that mathematical sciences were an exception because Ḥunayn did not master them, contrary to his optimal translations in other fields with which he was familiar, such as medicine, natural science, and metaphysics.[78] This means that the approach of translation was intertwined with the translator's knowledge of the content. There is more evidence on that. According to Muhammad Abdelraouf Awni, when official translation started at the time of al-Manṣūr (753–74 CE), many translators lacked the sufficient background knowledge to grasp metaphysical and philosophical thoughts, so they deleted whatever was difficult to comprehend and filled the gap with rationalist additions, so the

[77] Within a linguistic approach to translation, a unit of translation can be defined as "the minimal stretch of language that has to be translated together, as one unit" (Peter Newmark. *A Textbook of Translation* (New York: Prentice-Hall International, 1988), p. 54). In other words, it is "a unit in the source text for which an equivalent can be found in the text of the translation but whose elements, taken separately, do not correspond to equivalents in the translated text" (Leonid Barkhudarov. "The Problem of the Unit of Translation." In *Translation as Social Action: Russian and Bulgarian Perspectives*, edited by Palma Zlateva and Andre Lefevere (London: Routledge, 1993), p. 40). Barkhudarov's definition of the unit of translation responds, of course, to al-Ṣafadī's criticism of the word-for-word approach. Within a descriptive process-oriented approach to translation, the unit of translation can be defined as "the smallest source language text segments that are translated at one time" (Hans P. Krings, *Repairing Texts: Empirical Investigations of Machine Translation Post-Editing Processes*, edited by Geoffrey S. Koby (Kent, OH: The Kent State University Press, 2001), p. 80). The second definition clearly refers to the capacity of the translator as a language user.

[78] Rosenthal, *The Classical Heritage in Islam Arabic Thought and Culture*, pp. 17, 18. This difference in the quality of Ḥunayn's translations is also confirmed by al-Ṣafadī in his general short description of the two approaches to translation.

reader would not notice the loss. They also used transliteration, since Arabic, at that time, lacked technical terminology.[79]

Similarly, in a note on one of his translations, Ḥunayn stressed the importance of familiarity with the author's style and ideas. He was translating a Syriac translation of Galen into Arabic. Since he was familiar with the ideas and language of Galen, he could produce a good translation that even contributed to the quality of the original manuscript without experiencing problems with the translation. However, in a portion of the manuscript in which Galen quotes Aristophanes, Ḥunayn encountered a problem, since he was not familiar with Aristophanes' language and ideas. To aggravate the problem, the quotation contained a large number of mistakes, leaving Ḥunayn with only one option, which was to omit the quotation – it did not add much meaning to the manuscript anyway, according to Ḥunayn's evaluation.[80] Ḥunayn says,

> The Greek manuscript, from which I translated this work into Syriac, contains such a large number of mistakes and errors that it would have been impossible for me to understand the meaning of the text had I not been so familiar with and accustomed to Galen's Greek speech and acquainted with most of his ideas from his other works. But I am not familiar with the language of Aristophanes, nor am I accustomed to it. Hence, it was not easy for me to understand the quotation, and I have, therefore, omitted it. I had an additional reason for omitting it. After I had read it, I found no more in it than what Galen had already said elsewhere. Hence, I thought that I should not occupy myself with it any further, but rather proceed to more useful matters.[81]

Of course, omission is the worst option, but it could be an acceptable solution if we take into consideration how Ḥunayn reached his decision. Reading that quotation carefully, Ḥunayn decided that what was mentioned in the quotation was explained by Galen somewhere else, so it was redundant. As a result, Ḥunayn did not want to spend more time on that quotation and wanted to proceed to more important matters.

Translation as a developmental process, in which translators learn through translation, explains another significant feature of Arabic translation in the medieval period, that is, the continuous process of revision and retranslation.[82] For example, as we mentioned earlier, Galen's book on the

---

79 Awni, *Tārīkh al-tarjama al-ʿArabiyya bayna al-Sharq al-ʿarabi wa al-Gharb al-ʾŪrubi*, p. 49.

80 Rosenthal, *The Classical Heritage in Islam Arabic Thought and Culture*, p. 19.

81 Rosenthal, *The Classical Heritage in Islam Arabic Thought and Culture*, p. 19.

82 Translation at an early age, when the translator was still learning the foreign language, was similar to what Susan Bassnett calls "pedagogical translation" (Susan Bassnett. "Translation and Ideology." *Koiné, Annali della Scuola Superiore per Interpreti e Traduttori 'San Pellegrino'*, vol. 1, no. 2, 1991, pp. 7–32). In her article "Translation and Ideology," Susan Bassnett identifies three types of translation: pedagogical translation, poetic translation, and commercial translation. Pedagogical translation refers to translation activities in language teaching contexts, in

sects was translated and corrected at least three times by Ḥunayn Ibn Isḥāq. He first translated it into Syriac when he was in his early twenties. At that time, he had only one damaged Greek manuscript. When he was in his forties, he was able to collect more manuscripts, so he started correcting his early Syriac translation. A few years later, he translated the Syriac manuscript into Arabic for Abū Jaʿfar Muḥammad ibn Mūsa.[83]

Galen's *Book on the Methods of Healing* is another example. That book was translated into Syriac by Sergius. The first six books of that manuscript were badly translated, since Sergius, at that time, was still young. Later, he translated the remaining eight books, and the translation was far better than that of the earlier six books. Ḥunayn subsequently went on to collect a few manuscripts for the final eight books and he produced a fresh translation. For the first six books, he also came across one more manuscript and he also retranslated them, but they were still not as optimal as the final eight books. These translations were into Syriac, from which Ḥubaysh ibn al-Ḥasan produced a translation into Arabic, which he asked Ḥunayn to go through and correct.

Translation as Practical Decision-Making

Choosing a translation approach in the medieval Arabic translation movement was a complicated process of decision-making that was affected by a plethora of factors, such as language proficiency, knowledge of the content, and the purpose of translation. For example, scholars generally agree that two methods of translation, first described by al-Ṣafadī (1296–1363 CE), were used in the Graeco-Arabic translation movement.[84] The first – used by Yūḥannā ibn al-Baṭrīq, Ibn al-Nāʿima al-Ḥimṣī, and others – is a word-for-word translation in

which the focus is not on equivalence or communication but on ensuring that the student carries out a correct linguistic analysis of the source text and reflects this analysis in the way she synthesizes the target text. Thus, while some English passives are best rendered into the active voice in Arabic, it might be a good strategy in translation-based language classes to render the passive into passive to reflect an awareness of the structure in the source text. To the opposite extreme of pedagogical translation, poetic translation carries out changes to meet the expectations of target readers. For example, "Madame de la Motte . . . simply erased half of *The Iliad* because she said it wouldn't be very interesting to contemporary readers. Commercial translation began when there was a need to print books for a bigger market of readers. When original composition was unable to satisfy that need, commercial translation filled the gap. This explains why the seventeenth- and eighteenth-century theater in England was dominated by translations." These three kinds of translations can explain aspects of Arabic translation in the medieval period, but they do not cover the whole tradition. In particular, they cannot explain new thought added to translation. See Bassnett, "Translation and Ideology."

83 Rosenthal, *The Classical Heritage in Islam Arabic Thought and Culture*, p. 20.

84 See Ṣalāḥ al-Din Khalīl ibn Aybak Al-Ṣafadī. *Al-Ghayth al-*musajjam *fī sharḥ lāmiyyat al-ʿajam* (Syria, n.d.), pp. 1, 46. See also Rosenthal, *The Classical Heritage in Islam Arabic Thought and Culture*, pp. 17, 18, and Vagelpohl, *Aristotle's Rhetoric in the East*.

which each Greek word has a corresponding Arabic word as an equivalent.[85] The second method – followed as commonly stated by Ḥunayn ibn Isḥāq, al-Jawharī, and others – is a sense-for-sense translation in which a whole unit of meaning, be it a phrase or a whole clause, is rendered in the target language.[86]

The distinction between these two approaches within the Graeco-Arabic translation movement is a false dichotomy. To begin with, Hellenist-Arabists such as Fritz Zimmermann, Peter Adamson, and Dimitri Gutas have already analyzed various Arabic translations and confirmed that the translations hardly fit into one or the other of al-Ṣafadī's descriptions.[87] Peter Pormann compares translations by Ḥunayn ibn Isḥāq (as an example of al-Ṣafadī's sense-for-sense approach) and Ibn al-Biṭrīq (as an example of the word-for-word approach according to al-Ṣafadī) and concludes that "al-Ṣafadī's typology of translation owes more to an elegant idea than a concrete reality."[88] Similarly, John Nicholas Mattock compares two versions of Aristotle's *Metaphysics* – an earlier one ascribed to Usṭāth and another ascribed to Isḥāq ibn Ḥunayn – and finds that the translators behaved similarly as both "are far more at ease when the original is comparatively simple, and they are far more constricted by the individual words and phrases when it is more complex."[89]

Generally speaking, many changes were carried out to make the work easier to understand. Thus, changes such as omissions and reorganizations were not expected to result in gaps in the translated work. For example, Avicenna's commentary of the *Qiyās* mostly changed the organization of its source, Aristotle's *Prior Analytics*, but this did not divert Avicenna's attention from covering most of the material. Similarly, Avicenna did not actually omit Book IV of *Metaphysics*. He reorganized and presented the material somewhere else.[90]

---

[85] Problems with this literal method are easy to speculate. It is difficult to find an equivalent for every word, the resultant structure may violate the rules of the target language, the contextual meaning is usually ignored, and the output may be incomprehensible.

[86] According to Franz Rosenthal, this method is superior, and it was used by Ḥunayn ibn Isḥāq in most of his works.

[87] Peter E. Pormann. "The Development of Translation Techniques from Greek into Syriac and Arabic: The Case of Galen's *On the Faculties and Powers of Simple Drugs, Book Six*." In *Medieval Arabic Thought: Essays in Honour of Fritz Zimmermann*, edited by Rotraud E. Hansberger, Muhammad A. al-Akiti, Charles S. F. Burnett, and Fritz W. Zimmermann (London: Warburg Institute, 2012).

[88] Pormann, "The Development of Translation Techniques from Greek into Syriac and Arabic," p. 155.

[89] John N. Mattock. "The Early Translations from Greek into Arabic: An Experiment in Comparative Assessment." In *Symposium Graeco-Arabicum II: Akten des Zweiten Symposium Graeco-Arabicum*, Ruhr-Universität Bochum, 3–5 March (1989), pp. 73–102.

[90] Allan Bäck. "Avicenna the Commentator." In *Medieval Commentaries on Aristotle's Categories*, edited by Lloyd Newton (Leiden: Brill, 2008), p. 32.

Translation as Access to Its Source

One significant feature of the Graeco-Arabic translation movement is the more reliable access it provided to the long-perished Greek manuscripts, and the only access to them was through translation. That was possible because many of these translations were of earlier Greek manuscripts that were lost or suffered alterations in later centuries. For example, when Ernst Wenkebach attempted to edit the Greek text of Galen's commentary on Hippocrates' *Epidemics*, he reported that the Greek manuscripts, none of which predated the fourteenth century, suffered from numerous defects, including the loss of entire books. In addition, successive textual improvements and additions made the task of tracing the Greek original almost impossible. As a result, Wenkebach depended on Ḥunayn ibn Isḥāq's Arabic translation to accomplish his goal. Ḥunayn's translation, as Wenkebach confirms, is not only older than any of the extant Greek manuscripts but also more complete.[91] Similarly, Lourus Filius, the editor of an edition of the Arabic version of Aristotle's *Historia Animalium*, states that a valuable aspect of the Arabic translation is that it was a translation of a Greek manuscript that is older than any of the Greek manuscripts extant today; hence, it constitutes a valuable source for the establishment of the original Greek text.[92]

In addition, the Arabic translators paid great respect to their source texts. This is clear from their editing and translation strategies. To begin with, the translators did not ignore the multiple manuscripts available to them. In his *Risāla*, Ḥunayn Ibn Isḥāq gives us a clear idea of the value of each manuscript available to him. For example, he translated Galen's *De Sectis* when he was in his twenties from a damaged Greek manuscript. When he was in his forties, he had already collected a few manuscripts of the same text. He compared these versions and collated one correct manuscript. He then compared the Greek revised manuscript with a Syriac translation that was available to him, and he corrected it. Ḥunayn told us that this process of comparison and collation was his habit in all of the manuscripts that he translated.[93]

91 As Vagelpohl concludes, "the *Epidemics* strongly confirms the importance of the Arabic tradition for the reconstruction of this text and large sections of Greek medical literature more generally, a fact Wenkebach and also his predecessors were clearly aware of and that still applies to most of the Greek medical texts that survive in both their original language and in an Arabic tradition" (Vagelpohl, "Galen, *Epidemics*, Book One: Text, Transmission, Translation," pp. 129–30).

92 The manuscripts available for Aristotle's *Historia Animalium* are one from the ninth century and a few from the fourteenth century, all of which suffered so many alterations that tracking down Aristotle's original text is impossible. Part of the value of the Arabic translation of that text is that it was a translation of a manuscript that was much older than the oldest one extant today. Lourus S. Filius. *The Arabic Version of Aristotle's Historia Animalium: Book I–X of Kitāb al-Hayawān* (Leiden: Brill, 2018), pp. 3–4.

93 Isḥāq, *Risālat Ḥunayn ibn Isḥāq*, p. 5.

Unlike Ḥunayn, al-Ḥasan ibn Suwār ibn al-Khammār (943 to after 1017 CE), who belonged to the tenth-century philosophical school, whose members knew Arabic and Syriac, but not Greek, followed a more careful procedure. In his treatment of the *Sophistici Elenchi*, ibn al-Khammār says, "Since we like to inform ourselves about the share of each of the previous translators, we have written out all the three versions which fell into our hands so that they can all be studied and help mutually towards the understanding of the meaning."[94] The three versions that Ibn al-Khammār was referring to were three translations by three different translators: Yaḥyā ibn ʿAdī, ʿĪsā ibn Zurʿa, and Ibn Nāʿima al-Ḥimṣī. As Ibn al-Khammār says, he studied these three manuscripts, but he did not provide the reader with a definite text. Instead, he offered, in the margin or interlineally, all textual variants available to him.

Further, a rigorous and sustainable process of revision contributed to the quality of translations and made them closer to the source text. As we understand from *Risāla*, the revision of older translations was a common practice in the Graeco-Arabic translation movement. Some translations were so deviant or unreadable that new translations had to replace the old ones, such as Galen's treatises on the dissection of living and dead animals that was translated by Ayyūb al-Ruhāwī (760–840 CE). As Ḥunayn says in his *Risāla*, these translations were too difficult to correct, so he decided to translate them again. Some other translations were able to be revised, such as Galen's treatise on the motions of the blood in the heart and lungs, which was translated by Iṣṭifan ibn Basīl and revised by Ḥunayn.[95] That process of revision was continued by later translators, such as Ibn al-Khammār. There is also evidence that these revisions were strict. As Richard Walzer indicates, Ibn al-Kammār added notes whenever a word was added, deleted, or changed, and whenever there were textual variants.[96]

Translation as Problem-Solving

The Arabic translators used various techniques to solve linguistic translation problems at the word, phrase, and sentence levels. Such problems resulted from various factors, such as the purpose of translation, the nature of the process of translation itself, the translator's preferences, or the linguistic and cultural differences between the Greek and Syriac languages, on the one hand, and Arabic, on the other. These strategies can also be analyzed as yielding reader-oriented

94 Richard Walzer. "New Light on the Arabic Translations of Aristotle." *Oriens*, vol. 6, no. 1, 1953, p. 112.
95 Isḥāq, *Risālat Ḥunayn ibn Isḥāq*, pp. 23–7.
96 Walzer, "New Light on the Arabic Translations of Aristotle."

translations by carrying out a few functions, such as clarifying the text for the reader and smoothing transitions.

An important point to stress is that, although the following examples are taken from a limited number of texts and translators, they give us an idea of the techniques of the Arabic medieval translation at large.[97] The same remark is noted by Glen Cooper in his chapter titled "Ḥunayn Ibn Isḥāq and the Creation of an Arabic Galen."[98] Cooper analyzed Ḥunayn's translations of Galen's *On Crises* and *On Critical Days*, classifying Ḥunayn's translation techniques into four main categories: (a) expansions such as translating one Greek term into two Arabic words; (b) adding context or explanations, such as filling an information gap based on his knowledge of Galen's other works; (c) defining a term when it is not familiar to the readers or transliterating a term when it is familiar and does not need explanation; and (d) deliberate (mis)translations to accommodate the religious beliefs of the readers, such as translating the names of the Greek gods to Allah. According to Cooper, these strategies seem to be typical of Ḥunayn's translations, and they turn them into "a creative reading, an expansion on the Greek texts, with the primary aim of utility for research and medical practice, with the readers' needs at the forefront."[99]

Terminology

To solve the lexical problem of equivalence in the Arabic language, Iṣṭifan ibn Basīl, the first translator of the book of Dioscorides, employed two strategies. For the drugs that he knew, the problem was to derive equivalent Arabic names, which he did successfully. For the drugs that he did not know, the problem was doubled. It was not simply a problem of naming, since Iṣṭifan ibn Basīl had to make sure that the physician who read the book would administer the correct drug. Hence, Iṣṭifan ibn Basīl did not translate those Greek names and left them for later translators who might know the drugs. In this case, the translator's strategies were contingent on not only his language proficiency but also his expertise as a physician.

Another strategy to solve lexical problems is to define a term instead of translating it, which was frequently used by Ḥunayn ibn Ishāq in his medical

[97] As Uwe Vagelpohl comments on his research, "while these examples are all drawn from a single translation, the phenomenon they illustrate can be observed in a large number of texts associated with the translation workshop of Ḥunayn ibn Isḥāq" (Uwe Vagelpohl. "The User-Friendly Galen: Ḥunayn ibn Isḥāq and the Adaptation of Greek Medicine for a New Audience." In *Greek Medical Literature and Its Readers: From Hippocrates to Islam and Byzantium*, edited by Petros Bouras-Vallianatos and Sophia Xenophontos (London: Routledge, 2018), p. 119).

[98] Glen M. Cooper. "Ḥunayn Ibn Isḥāq and the Creation of an Arabic Galen." In *Brill's Companion to the Reception of Galen*, edited by Petros Bouras-Vallianatos and Barbara Zipser (Leiden: Brill, 2019), pp. 179–95.

[99] Cooper, "Ḥunayn Ibn Isḥāq and the Creation of an Arabic Galen."

translations. For example, instead of translating "epidemic diseases" into two words, Ḥunayn substituted it with a definition: "the same disease that affects a large group at the same time and in the same area contrary to what the inhabitants of that area are accustomed to." Similarly, he replaced "mesentery" with "the regions between the bowels and the membrane that covers them." Sometimes, instead of translating, Ḥunayn provided an explanation or a gloss. For example, he translated "the future diseases" into "the diseases that will occur are usual general diseases or similar ones that are, unlike this one, benign and harmless."[100]

Compounds and Connecting Articles

More linguistic-oriented problems include the Greek compounds and connecting articles. In the following text, Ḥunayn ibn Isḥāq modified his target text because the Arabic language lacked an equivalent to the Greek system of compounds:

> من خاصة البدن الصحيح ألا يكون به وجع، وسواء قلت في هذا الموضع "وجع" أو "ألم" أو "أذى."
>
> One characteristic of a healthy body is that it is free of pain, regardless of whether I say "pain," "ache," or "suffering" in this place.

The Greek text includes compounds with negative particles to indicate the opposite or absence of a characteristic. Since Arabic lacks the same mechanism, the translator negated the whole sentence, "*allā yakūn bi-hi wajaʿ*" ("free of pain, suffers no pain"). Then being unable to use compounds with negative particles with the other two nouns, the translator explained that the negation applies to the other words – "no ache" and "no suffering."[101]

In his chapter "Galen, *Epidemics*, Book One: Text, Transmission, Translation," Uwe Vagelpohl analyzes the Greek and Arabic systems of connecting particles as an example of how differences between the two linguistic systems, as well as the translator's preferences, may affect translation.[102]

The Greek connecting particles are different from their Arabic equivalents, as the Greek particles are more complicated. To analyze and translate which meaning and function is conveyed by the Greek particle, the Arabic translator may choose between a variety of Arabic expressions with similar meaning and function, so, as Vagelpohl indicates, the selection usually depends on the translator's preference.

---

[100] Vagelpohl, "The User-Friendly Galen," pp. 119–20.

[101] Vagelpohl, *Galeni In Hippocratis Epidemiarum Librum I Commentariorum I–III Versionem Arabicam/Galen.*

[102] Vagelpohl, "Galen, *Epidemics*, Book One."

Double Translation

Double translation, hendiadys, or synonymic doublets (translating one source lexical item using two words in the target language) are used to clarify the meaning of the source text and to accommodate various readers. This strategy is perhaps the most recurrent strategy in translations from Greek and Syriac into Arabic. It is used by both the more competent and the less competent translators.

According to Vagelpohl, these hendiadyses are usually used as a stylistic device, as they are used to translate unproblematic terms.[103] This is very true when we consider a hendiadys such as "remember and keep in mind." This is also supported by the fact that hendiadyses are the most frequent stylistic feature not only in Ḥunayn's translations but also in others' translations, such as of Abū Bishr Mattā. However, hendiadyses carry out a few other functions. For example, the hendiadys "dry and devoid of rain" was used for emphasis, as it commonly is in Arabic. Immediately before that hendiadys, the translator paraphrased and amplified a Greek statement by repeating elements from the previous sentence and the lemma, stating that Hippocrates "expressed himself differently than usual because when we say that one of the seasons was 'dry and devoid of rain,' our observation would normally be understood to mean that it was extremely dry so that there was no rain at all during it." To emphasize the "extremely dry weather," the translator used the two adjectival phrases "dry and devoid of rain." Similarly, the following hendiadyses were more likely used for emphasis: "of every country and every community," "each country and each community," "fortify them, strengthen them," and "intensifies and increases it," among others. Other hendiadyses, such as "minor, specific," "observes and investigates," "deduce and know well," "reliable and regular," and "is strong and predominates" may reflect the translator's doubts that one word may not be precise enough.

Greek Pronominal References and Use of Personal Forms

Due to syntactic differences between Greek and Arabic, replacing Greek pronominal references with noun referents is recurrent in Arabic translations. For example, in his medical translations, Ḥunayn ibn Isḥāq sometimes rendered "he describes" into "Hippocrates describes" to clarify the referent. This was done whether the subject was implicit, since Galen did not need to spell out the subject every time he spoke of Hippocrates, or when a pronominal reference was used instead of the proper noun.[104]

[103] All examples of double translation in this paragraph are borrowed from Vagelpohl, *Galeni In Hippocratis Epidemiarum Librum I Commentariorum I–III Versionem Arabicam/Galen*, and Vagelpohl, "The User-Friendly Galen."

[104] Vagelpohl, "The User-Friendly Galen," pp. 119–20.

In her article "Subjectivity in Translation," Elaine van Dalen compares nearly all personal forms in Galen's commentary on the Hippocratic *Aphorisms* and its Arabic translation and concludes that Ḥunayn ibn Isḥāq's translation is significantly more personal than Galen's commentary.[105] According to her analysis, Ḥunayn's personal forms were employed to achieve five semantic functions: (a) the personal expression of stance, (b) frame-marking, (c) endophoric reference, (d) the expression of personal opinion, and (e) the impersonal expression of intersubjectivity. The final three functions are significant to our purpose. Endophoric forms such as "I have shown" and "we will discuss later" have a cohesive function, and they contribute to the smoothness of the text. Similarly, some additions, such as "after this . . . he said," "in spite of this," "namely that," and "in view of this it is therefore appropriate that" are intended to smooth transition and enhance the text clarity.[106]

Another important function of the use of personal forms is the expression of personal opinion. When personal forms are used for that purpose, they not only mark the passage as new thought added by the translators but also make the text reader-friendly. In addition, Ḥunayn used personal forms to express intersubjectivity. For example, in his translation of the *Epidemics*, it happened occasionally that Ḥunayn changed the first-person plural to the first-person singular. The plural pronoun might be confusing to Arabic readers, especially when it might refer to both Hippocrates and Galen, but the use of the first-person singular turned the text personal and reader-oriented.[107] Similarly, in his translation of Galen's commentary on the Hippocratic *Aphorisms*, Ḥunayn substituted "you" for "us," thus marking the text as shared information between the author and reader.[108] All of these strategies imply an active process of translation in which the translator tries to understand the text and make it clear to the reader.

Domestication, Christianization, and Islamization

Ḥunayn was prone to domesticate foreign references. For example, in his translation of the *Epidemics*, he changed "barley porridge," a Greek dish unknown to his Arab readers, to "barley cake."[109]

---

[105] Elaine van Dalen's main argument is that, although Ḥunayn used more personal forms, his translation is not necessarily more subjective than Galen's text (Elaine van Dalen. "Subjectivity in Translation: Ḥunayn ibn Isḥāq's Ninth-Century Interpretation of Galen's 'Ego' in his *Commentary on the Hippocratic Aphorisms*." *Oriens*, vol. 45, 2017, pp. 53–79).

[106] See Vagelpohl, *Galeni In Hippocratis Epidemiarum Librum I Commentariorum I–III Versionem Arabicam/Galen.*

[107] See Vagelpohl, *Galeni In Hippocratis Epidemiarum Librum I Commentariorum I–III Versionem Arabicam/Galen.*

[108] Dalen, "Subjectivity in Translation," p. 76.

[109] I am indebted, for all of the examples from the *Epidemics*, to Uwe Vagelpohl. See Vagelpohl, *Galeni In Hippocratis Epidemiarum Librum I Commentariorum I–III Versionem Arabicam/ Galen.*

Likewise, in several examples, when the translator was faced with the name of a place or a person that his Arab readers may not have been familiar with, he added phrases that would assist in recognizing the reference. Examples include "the place called Hellespontos" and "the place called Cranon," where "the place called" was added to clarify that it was the name of a geographical area. Similarly, when Galen explained that the term "epidemics" was written in some copies with four syllables and in others with five syllables, Ḥunayn transferred the Greek metalanguage into Arabic metalanguage, explaining that *ibīdīmya* was sometimes written with seven letters (إبيذيمي) and sometimes with eight (إبيذيمين).

Another characteristic of the Arabic translation is how the translators alleviated the pagan character of the foreign texts. For example, in his translation of the *Epidemics*, Ḥunayn frequently adapted the polytheistic references to monotheistic beliefs.[110] In his chapter "Galen the Pagan and Ḥunayn the Christian," Gotthard Strohmaier analyzes a good number of examples in which Ḥunayn adapted pagan references to the Christian and Muslim worldview.[111] The strategy is not specific to Ḥunayn, as Gotthard Strohmaier observes that similar strategies were used by eastern Christians in their Syriac translations from Greek, as well as in Muslim translations from Pahlavi. A number of scenarios, which are not mutually exclusive, can explain such a strategy. The Christian translators might not have wanted to raise Muslim suspicions that they would introduce pagan beliefs under the cover of Greek science, they may not have wanted to upset their Christian readers, or they may have wanted to comply with the literary tastes of their sponsors.[112] The first reason is significant, since we have seen how Abū Bishr Mattā was severely criticized for supporting the Greek logic against Arabic grammar; it truly depicts the sensitivity of the Muslim community to paganism and Hellenization. However, the three reasons given by Strohmaier refer strongly to a reader-oriented approach to translation whether the purpose was to satisfy their Christian or Muslim readers or to satisfy their sponsors.

These changes are also significant because they imply a process of critical engagement with the source text. I borrow the following example from Gotthard Strohmaier.[113] In his translation of a passage from a commentary on the

110 See Vagelpohl, *Galeni In Hippocratis Epidemiarum Librum I Commentariorum I–III Versionem Arabicam/Galen*.

111 Gotthard Strohmaier. "Galen the Pagan and Ḥunayn the Christian: Specific Transformations in the Commentaries on *Airs, Waters, Places* and the *Epidemics*." In *Epidemics in Context: Greek Commentaries on Hippocrates in the Arabic Tradition*, edited by Peter E. Pormann (Berlin: De Gruyter, 2012), pp. 171–84.

112 Strohmaier, "Galen the Pagan and Ḥunayn the Christian."

113 Strohmaier, "Galen the Pagan and Ḥunayn the Christian," pp. 172–3.

Hippocratic Oath, Ḥunayn uses a metaphorical interpretation to translate and explain the myth that Zeus killed Asclepius with a lightning bolt because the latter raised a man from the dead, thus challenging the immortality of the gods. Ḥunayn changed the pagan references in his translation:

> وذلك أن الأقاويل التي نجدها مكتوبة في تألهه إنما تليق بالخرافات لا بالحق. ومن المشهور من أمره أنه رفع إلى الملائكة في عمود من النار، كما يقال في زيونوسس وإرقلس وسائر من أشبههما ممن عني بنفع الناس واجتهد في ذلك. وبالجملة يقال إن الله تبارك وتعالى فعل بأسقليبيوس وسائر من اشبهه هذا الفعل، كيما يفنى الجزء الميت الأرضي منه النار، ثم يجتذب بعد ذلك جزءه الذي لا يقبل الموت ويرفع نفسه إلى السماء.

> The written accounts that we find about his [sc. Asclepius'] deification are more like idle talk than the truth. It is a well-known fact that he was raised to the angels in a column of fire. The same is also said about Dionysus and Heracles and similar men who work zealously for the benefit of mankind. In general, God, blessed and exalted, is said to have done this with Asclepius and all the others like him in order to destroy his mortal earthly part through fire and, afterwards, attract his immortal part and raise his soul to heaven.

In a note on the passage, Ḥunayn explains:

> جالينوس في هذا الموضع يبين كيف يكون تشبه الإنسان بالله تبارك وتعالى وذلك أنه يقول إن الإنسان إذا أباد شهواته الجسمانية بالنار والصبر والإمساك عنها وهي التي يريد بها "جزءه الميت الأرضي" وزين نفسه الناطقة بعد النفي من هذه الشهوات
> بالفضائل وهي التي يريد' بها "الارتفاع إلى السماء" كان شبيها بالله تبارك وتعالى.

> Galen explains here how man can become more similar to God, blessed and exalted. He says that when a human being annihilates his bodily desires – this is what he means by "his mortal earthly part" – through the fire of endurance and abstention, and adorns his rational soul, after driving it away from those desires, with virtues – this is what he means by "raised to heaven" – he becomes similar to God, blessed and exalted.

Applying such a "cultural filter" on the Greek texts is probably the only example of replacement.[114] I am not saying that adapting the Greek beliefs to Islam and Christianity, the symbolic interpretation, or the changes carried out in the translation are either fair or not true to the source text, but I am referring to an important process that took place throughout the Arabic medieval translation movement, namely the critical and creative engagement with the source text, a process that eventually led to the introduction of Islamic philosophy by Avicenna.

Therefore, the Islamization of Greek texts resulted in two kinds of changes. The first change was carried out at the word, phrase, or sentence level where

[114] The term is borrowed from Juliane House. *A Model for Translation Quality Assessment* (Tübingen, Germany: Gunter Narr Verlag, 1977).

substitution, deletion, or addition could solve the problem. The second change was carried out at the level of ideas, and it usually involved greater creativity than the first change. The best example is the creation of *ʿilm al-hayʾah* (علم الهيئة, the science of configuration or astronomy) by the eleventh century. Muslim scholars and philosophers questioned the assumptions of astrology not only because astrological predictions could be wrong but also because they threatened God's unity. As a result, Muslim scholars created a new field of astronomy that examined the positions of the planets, leaving aside the significance and influence of those positions on the world to another field that came to be known as *ʿilm aḥkām al-nujūm* (the science of the judgments of the stars or astrology).[115]

In this section, some important characteristics of the Arabic translation movement have been discussed, but the classical claim – that the value of the medieval Arabic translation constitutes the preservation of Greek sciences until they are rediscovered in Europe – has not been challenged much so far. In fact, the characteristics outlined earlier – which I see as strengths rather than weaknesses – confirm, rather than challenge, that narrative. Unlike the Romans, who displaced the Greek texts, the Arabic translators respected their sources and paid painstaking attention to conveying their complete meaning. The work of the Arabic translators, along with their manuscript collation efforts and rigorous translation revisions, enabled the Latin scholars to later establish the Greek originals from the Arabic. However, this only partially explains the Arabic translation movement. Another equally significant narrative is how the Arabic translators added new thoughts to their sources by engaging with them critically and creatively, as we will explore in the next section.

[115] See Robert Morrison. "Astronomy." In *Medieval Islamic Civilization: An Encyclopedia*, edited by Joseph Meri and Jere Bacharach (London: Routledge, 2006), p. 78.

6 Toward a Definition of Arabic Translation in the Medieval Period

Given the huge span of time covered by the Arabic translation movement and the wide area of the Muslim Empire where translation was practiced, some scholars argue that there is no coherent body of theories to explain the whole Graeco-Arabic translation movement. This is because of the considerable variation in the practice[116] and because the medieval intellectuals rarely discussed the work of the translators.[117] In spite of that, there is a common theme among all medieval Arabic translations that is almost absent from the literature, namely the use of Arabic translation as a means of knowledge production. Only when we start looking at medieval Arabic translations from this perspective can a coherent body of theories appear to connect all of them. As a means of knowledge production, the most important feature of translation is the critical and creative engagement with the source text.

Translation as creative engagement with the source text is supported by the original meaning of the Arabic word *tarjam* (to translate). Morphologically speaking, the term *tarjam* is either from the root *rajm*, meaning "to throw stones at"[118] or "to guess,"[119] or from the quadrilateral root *tarjam*, which has a few meanings, two of them relating to translation: "to explain speech in another language" and "to explain one's own speech in the same language." These definitions are significant because they indicate that translation is not used in Arabic to refer to saying the same thing in another language. According to these definitions, translation refers to explaining, elaborating, or clarifying. That attitude toward translation, namely as explanation, was the most dominant approach during the Graeco-Arabic translation movement. Thus, various nouns such as *naql* (transfer) and *taʿrīb* (Arabization), and verbs such as *sharaḥ* (to explain) and *fassar* (to interpret), are used by Arabic writers in the medieval period to refer to translation activities.[120]

[116] For example, some of these translations are reader-oriented and written in an easy-to-grasp style, whereas some attempt to shadow the source text word by word. Some translations, as we read in Ḥunayn's *Risāla*, are functionalists, as they are influenced by their purpose, that is, whether they are produced for a fellow philosopher, a junior scholar, or the public.

[117] Uwe Vagelpohl. "The Abbasid Translation Movement in Context: Contemporary Voices on Translation." In *Abbasid Studies II. Occasional Papers of the School of Abbasid Studies. Leuven, 28 June–1 July 2004*, edited by John Nawas (Leuven: Peeters, 2010), pp. 245–67.

[118] As in Qur'ān 11:91, "*wa lawlā rahṭuka larajamnāka*" ("and if not for your family, we would have stoned you").

[119] As in Qur'ān 18:22, "*rajman bi al-ghayb*" ("guessing at the unseen").

[120] See Myriam Salama-Carr. "Medieval translators into Arabic – Scribes or Interpreters?" In *Beyond the Western Tradition*, edited by Marilyn Gaddis Rose (New York: State University of New York at Binghamton), p. 102. Myriam Salama-Carr and Theo Hermans. "Translation into Arabic in the 'Classical' Age: When the Pandora's Box of Transmission opens." *Translating Others*, vol. 1, 2006, pp. 121–31.

The development of the meaning of "translation" from explanation, as used in the medieval period, to the rendition of equivalent meaning, as used in modern standard Arabic, points to the evolution of the Arab mind and its intellectual activities, since "in the birth of individual words and the stages of their growth could be discovered the stages of evolution of the human mind."[121] Indeed, medieval Arabic translation involved critical and creative engagement, whereas contemporary Arabic translation has imprisoned the translator in producing an equivalent to the source text.

In the contemporary theory of translation, imitation and originality are restricted to a few problem-solving techniques. For example, translators can choose to imitate the source text, translate it word for word, or focus on the sense and convey the meaning in a different packaging. Similarly, translators can choose to either imitate the source text – thus producing a highly foreignizing translation – or domesticate it by adapting it to the target culture. Such procedures have little or nothing to do with the content, since contemporary translators are not theoretically supported to modify, reorganize, or supplement the content. In contrast, medieval Arabic translators used strategies that are no longer considered part of the process of translation, such as adding new information to the target text or presenting old information in a new form.

The Arabic medieval translation can also be analyzed according to an imitation–innovation model. The Arabic translators highly respected their source texts and took them as models to imitate. That is why epitomes and commentaries were the most common forms of scientific writings. However, the Arabic translators did not blindly imitate those texts. In many instances, they criticized, corrected, and improved their source texts. In general terms, the Arabic translators and the Muslim scholars after them attempted to save the Greek writers from any contradiction, correcting whatever they found inconsistent with the writer's general ideas or approach. At the same time, their great respect for the Greek writers did not inhibit them from amending gaps and absurdities and adding new thought to the target text.

An important question to consider is whether adding original thought to translation coincides with medieval theory or violates its code. A quick survey of the criticisms that were addressed against translation indicates that translations were criticized for weak language or lack of clarity, but they were never criticized for adding fresh material to the source text. This means that the practice of improving and adding thought to the source text (i.e. creative engagement with the source text) was a common practice, and it was by no means aberrant to medieval Arabic translation standards.

[121] Timothy Mitchell. *Colonising Egypt* (Cambridge: Cambridge University Press, 1988), p. 139.

Creative Engagement with the Source Text

Creative engagement with the source text occurs at any text level, from a single word to a whole treatise. It also involves, by necessity, critical engagement with the source text, as it is based upon an initial assessment of the strengths and weaknesses of the source text. Thus, the strategies underlying creative engagement involve a sensible process of decision-making based on careful examination of the source text. Creative engagement with the source text includes selecting a textual variant; analyzing and criticizing the views of the source text or correcting its mistakes; deleting redundant and inauthentic passages, including additions to fill a gap in the content; reframing the content; and adding new thought to the target text.

Selecting a Textual Variant

When more than one manuscript is available to the translator, he faces the problem of textual variation. In this case, two strategies have been recorded in the Arabic translation tradition. Ḥunayn ibn Isḥāq collated the different manuscripts available to him, selecting and introducing, in his translation, the most convincing textual variant. The disadvantage of this method is that the manuscript loses part of its historical richness. By contrast, al-Ḥasan ibn Suwār ibn al-Khammār (943 to after 1017 CE) used a more flexible strategy, where he selected a variant while introducing other textual variants interlineally or in the margin.

In-text additions and comments, such as "We find that the copies disagree in this place," which is added by Ḥunayn ibn Isḥāq in his translation of the *Epidemics*,[122] are significant because they provide access to what was going on in the mind of the translator during the process of translation. Throughout history, translation theory has been prescriptive, consisting of rules outlining things that translators should or should not do. In the early twentieth century, the idea that scientific methodology could be applied to cultural products was developed by Russian formalists and, a few decades later, it was introduced in the field of translation studies with the works of Itamar Evan-Zohar and Gideon Toury.[123] At the same time, the psycholinguistic approach to translation offers scientific tools to examine the process of translation in actual time (i.e. what happens in the translator's mind during the process of translating). With this approach, it is claimed that the mental

[122] Vagelpohl, *Galeni In Hippocratis Epidemiarum Librum I Commentariorum I–III Versionem Arabicam/Galen*, p. 321.

[123] Itamar Even-Zohar. "Polysystem Studies." *Poetics Today*, vol. 11,no. 1, 1990, pp. 9–26. Gideon Toury. *In Search of a Theory of Translation* (Tel Aviv: Porter Institute for Poetics and Semiotics, Tel Aviv University, 1980).

process of translation is translators' black box, to which we have no direct access unless the translators tell us what is going on in their minds while translating – via retrospective accounts or the think-aloud protocols in which translators translate, speak aloud, and record all of their thoughts while translating.[124] These methods have developed to include eye tracking and recording keyboard tapping, but the idea is the same – to have access to the mental process of translating. Since this is not possible for translations produced centuries ago, the only valuable sources we can rely on to understand the mental process of translation are retrospective writings such as the *Risāla* of Ḥunayn ibn Isḥāq and in-text additions such as the one explained earlier.

Analyzing and Criticizing the Views of the Source Text or Correcting Its Mistakes

Creative engagement encompasses criticisms of the views of the source text. In his translation of the pseudo-Aristotelian *Physiognomics*, Ḥunayn uses his medical experience and knowledge to read the text critically. As Uwe Vagelpohl states, almost one-third of Ḥunayn's notes on that work criticizes or even rejects "the reasoning of the author."[125] In addition, creative engagement sometimes takes the form of correcting a mistake in a manuscript. For example, in his translation of Galen's *On the Capacities of Simple Drugs*, Ḥunayn ibn Isḥāq corrects "chasteberry seeds" to "flax seeds," indicating in a gloss that it was a copyist error.[126]

Similarly, in his translation of Ptolemy's *Almagest*, al-Ḥajjāj ibn Maṭar corrected Ptolemy's report about the length of the lunar month:

> In it Ptolemy says that he was simply following Hipparchus who had in turn taken two lunar eclipses that were separated by 126,007 days and 1 hour, during which the moon made 4,267 revolutions. Ptolemy went on to say that if one divided the number of days by the number of revolutions, that is, divided $126{,}007^{d}$ and 1^{h} by 4,267, one would get the length of the lunar month to be 29 days, 31 minutes, 50 seconds, 8 thirds, 20 fourths (or alternatively written as $29;31,50,8,20^{d}$). In fact if one were to carry out the division, as prescribed by Ptolemy, the answer would not be the one given in the Ptolemaic text, rather it would be $29;31,50, 8,9,20^{d}$, which is exactly the number found in the earliest surviving Arabic translation of the Almagest by al-Ḥajjāj.[127]

---

[124] See Roger T. Bell. *Translation and Translating: Theory and Practice* (New York: Longman, 1991).

[125] See Vagelpohl, "The User-Friendly Galen," p. 122.

[126] Vagelpohl, "The User-Friendly Galen," p. 121.

[127] Saliba, *Islamic Science and the Making of the European Renaissance*, pp. 79–80.

This might seem a simple textual correction, but it cannot be done under normal circumstances. It requires not only background knowledge but also an attitude to examine and utilize the source text knowledge. George Saliba analyzes this correction in terms of the competition among the scholars to master the advanced sciences, hence having access to higher positions in the administration. This also confirms that translation was not simply an act of communicating meaning, but also a means of engaging with the advanced sciences.

Deleting Redundant and Inauthentic Passages

Sometimes, textual engagement requires pervasive changes, such as deleting whole sections because the translator believes they were fabricated and added to the text later. Ḥunayn employed that strategy, but he was not the first one to do so. Before him, Galen frequently expressed his views on genuine Hippocratic writings and those that were added to it later. Being familiar with Hippocrates' views, Ḥunayn disqualified those writings that were at odds with the interpretation of Hippocrates' views, as is clear from the following quotation:

> ولم يقتصر المترجمون للكتب على هذا حتى أدخلوا في هذا الكتاب هذيانا كثيرا ووصفات بديعة عجيبة، وأدوية لم يرها جالينوس ولم يسمع بها . . . وسألني بعض أصدقائي أن أقرأ الكتاب السرياني وأصححه على حسب ما أرى أنه موافق رأي جالينوس ففعلت.
>
> The translators of the books were not content with this until they introduced into this book much drivel and marvelous and wonderous recipes, as well as drugs that Galen had not seen or even heard about . . . One of my friends asked me to read this Syriac book and correct it according to what I considered appropriate to the style of Galen, which I did.[128]

Ḥunayn also thought critically of his own translation strategies. We have seen above that he deleted Aristophanes' quotation in his Syriac into Arabic translation of Galen's *Medical Names* because the Greek manuscript from which he initially translated the Syriac was unclear, and the meaning of the deleted passage was explained somewhere else in the text. In his translation of Book 2 of the *Epidemics*, he explains that he thought of deleting a Greek passage because he was unable to reproduce its multilayered meaning. Depending on how to parse the Greek passage, the reader can understand different meanings – all conveyed by Galen previously in the text. That time, Ḥunayn reconsidered deleting the phrase, deciding it may still be useful for some readers:[129]

---

[128] Ḥunayn ibn Isḥāq. *Ḥunayn ibn Isḥāq on his Galen translations*, edited and translated by John C. Lamoreaux (Provo, UT: Brigham Young University Press, 2016), p. 88.

[129] See Vagelpohl, "The User-Friendly Galen," p. 122.

قال حنين: إن هذا الكلام في اللسان اليوناني محتمل لأنه يقطع ويقرأ على أنحاء شتى من التقطيع والقراءة فيدل بحسب كل واحد من أنواع تقطيعه وقراءته على واحد واحد من هذه المعاني التي أشار إليها جالينوس. وليس ذلك في العربية بممكن ولذلك قد كنت هممت بإسقاط هذا الكلام إذ كان لا يطابق اللغة العربية ويفهم فيها على حقوقها إلا أني لما وجدت معاني قد مرت في هذا الكلام نافعة لمن تدبرها رأيت ترجمته على حال إذ كانت ليس تضر ترجمته وهي إلى منفعة أقرب. ومن قرأ فقدر أن يصل إلى الانتفاع به فهو منه ربح ومن لم يقدر على ذلك فهو قادر أن يتاركه فلا يضره مكانه شيئا إن شاء الله.

Ḥunayn said: In the Greek this passage can be split up and read [i.e. parsed] in various ways. It signifies each separate meaning Galen pointed out depending on the particular ways it is split up and read. This is not possible in Arabic. Since this passage does not suit the Arabic language and could not be understood completely in it, I had considered dropping it but decided to translate it anyway when I found ideas in this passage that benefit the people who study them since translating it does not hurt but may rather be beneficial. Those who read it can draw [some] benefit and therefore profit from it; those who cannot may ignore it without suffering any harm, God willing.

Likewise, in a note on Book 6 of Galen's *Commentary on Hippocrates' Epidemics*, Ḥunayn explains that he deleted a passage not only because it posed a comprehension burden on the reader but also because it did not add anything valuable to the text.[130] He says:

اقتص جالينوس أقاويل من أقاويل أوميروس وأفلاطون وغيرهما من القدماء قد يدل على النسق فيها
ونسق الشيء على غير ما هو ملائم له ليس له في العربية
نظائر تحسن فتركت ترجمتها لأنه لا ينتفع بها في العربية . . .

Then, Galen related sayings by Homer, Plato, and others of the ancients in which he indicates that the [grammatical] congruence between them is inappropriate. In Arabic, there are no equivalents to it. I have, therefore, not translated them into Arabic as they are useless in Arabic . . .

Additions to Fill a Gap in the Content

When Ḥunayn added something to the body of his translation, it usually contributed to the content of the text, filling a gap or clarifying the meaning. As he says in a note in Book 2 of Galen's *Commentary on Hippocrates' Epidemics*:

فتكلفت استتمام ما نقص من عند نفسي بحسب ما رأيت جالينوس ينحو نحوه في
تفسير أشباه هذا الكلام وعلى الأصول التي أخذتها عنه من كتبه.

I took upon myself to fill the gap in accordance with what I thought was Galen's method in commenting on similar lemmas and according to the principles I took from his writings.

[130] I borrow this and the following example from Hallum, "The Arabic Reception of Galen's *Commentary on Hippocrates' 'Epidemics'*," p. 168.

Glen Cooper clarifies that one of the strategies that Ḥunayn employs in his translations is "adding context or explanation" based on his knowledge of Galen's style and ideas. For example, in:

> *On Critical Days*, when Galen is describing the symptoms that must occur in order to prevent the illness from returning, Ḥunayn adds: "so that when you see that the illness has abated without one of these two things occurring before it subsides", that is, you may be sure that the illness will return, since the patient has not experienced a full recovery.[131]

As Cooper explains, "this addition is consistent with Galenic crisis theory, and the physician is enjoined to watch for these crucial signs."[132]

Reframing the Content

Another type of creative engagement with the content is the addition of phrases that structure the content for the reader. Ḥunayn ibn Isḥāq's translation of the *Epidemics* is abundant with additions that give a sense of summary to the reader. Examples include, "there are two types," "these two kinds," "this fever is bad in two ways," "there are two reasons for this," "this takes the patient in one of two directions," and "there were two possible outcomes."[133]

Similarly, creative engagement with the content comprises presenting the source text content in different forms. In his *Risāla*, Ḥunayn refers to two forms of such engagement: exposition and epitome. Examples of expositions include his translation of Hippocrates' commentary on *Nutrition*. Ḥunayn says, "I translated it into Syriac for Salmawayh. I also translated the lemmata of Hippocrates's treatise [found] in this book and to it added a short exposition."[134] To his Syriac translation of *Commentary on Hippocrates's Oath*, he added his own exposition of the difficult passages. He also added a short exposition to his Syriac translation of *Commentary on Air, Water, and Places* that he did not manage to finish.

The most recurrent form of critical presentation is the epitome. For example, as Uwe Vagelpohl explains, Ḥunayn's audience was more interested in medical practice. To satisfy their needs, Ḥunayn summarized Galen's commentaries on Hippocratic writings to remove the "long and unwieldy" material irrelevant for therapeutic and prognostic practice.[135] Ḥunayn also wrote summaries extracted from the *Epidemics* in question-and-answer format. Two such summaries,

---

[131] Cooper, "Ḥunayn Ibn Isḥāq and the Creation of an Arabic Galen," p. 185.

[132] Cooper, "Ḥunayn Ibn Isḥāq and the Creation of an Arabic Galen," p. 185.

[133] All of these examples are marked as additions by the translator to the Greek text. They are not paraphrases or amplifications. See Vagelpohl, *Galeni In Hippocratis Epidemiarum Librum I Commentariorum I–III Versionem Arabicam/Galen*.

[134] Isḥāq, *Ḥunayn ibn Isḥāq on his Galen Translations*, p. 104.

[135] Vagelpohl, "The User-Friendly Galen," p. 123.

which are lost but referenced in other extant works, are *Fuṣūl Istakhrajahā min Kitāb Ibīdīmyā* (*Aphorisms Drawn from the* Epidemics) and *Masā'il fī al-Bawllintaza'ahā min Kitāb Ibīdīmyā li-Ibuqrāṭ* (*Questions on Urine Extracted from Hippocrates'* Epidemics). Ḥunayn also summarized Books 1, 2, and 3 of Hippocrates *Epidemics* under the title *Jawāmi' Ma'ānī al-Maqāla al-Ūlā wa-al-Thāniyaa wa-al-Thālitha min Kitāb Ibuqrāṭ 'ala Ṭarīq al-mas'ala wa-al-jawāb* (*Summaries of the Contents of Books 1, 2, and 3 of Hippocrates'* Epidemics *in the Form of Questions and Answers*).[136]

In his *Risāla*, Ḥunayn refers to some of these summaries. In his comment on Galen's *Decay*, he says, "I think that Job has translated it. As for me, I did not translate it. Rather, I extracted in tabular form its [essential] ideas (that is, its main points), along with [those of] some other volumes."[137] In his comment on *Authentic and Spurious Works of Hippocrates*, Ḥunayn states that he translated the volume into Syriac for 'Īsā ibn Yaḥyā and made an epitome of it.[138]

That practice of producing epitomes was developed by Averroes, who was known to produce three types of epitomes, each targeting a particular audience. For the public and nonspecialist readers, Averroes produced short summaries that were easily digestible and eased any discrepancies between Aristotle's and Muslim doctrines. For the learned who were not philosophers, he produced the middle commentary, and for the Muslim philosophers, he wrote the long commentaries. Other strategies of critical engagement with the content included reproducing the information in the form of tables and diagrams. These diagrams are known as the *tashjīr* genre, and Ḥunayn was among the first scholars to use it.[139] Although these fresh presentations are performed after translation, they are completely based on translation and are carried out by translators.

Another example of reframing the content is reorganizing a work and potentially choosing a different title. A good example is Ibrahim al-Fazārī's (d. 777 CE) translation of *Zīj al-Sindhind*, for which he changed the title and order of the chapters. We learn from the *Risāla* of Ḥunayn ibn Isḥāq that reorganizing a work was not uncommon in the Alexandrian school. One example is Galen's treatise on veins and arteries. As Ḥunayn says, "This book, according to Galen, consists of a single volume . . . As for the Alexandrians, they divided it into two volumes, one on veins and one on arteries."[140] In his comment on his translation

[136] Vagelpohl, *Galeni In Hippocratis Epidemiarum Librum I Commentariorum I–III Versionem Arabicam/Galen*, p. 35.
[137] Isḥāq, *Ḥunayn ibn Isḥāq on his Galen Translations*, p. 82.
[138] Isḥāq, *Ḥunayn ibn Isḥāq on his Galen Translations*, p. 108.
[139] See Vagelpohl, "The User-Friendly Galen," p. 124.
[140] Isḥāq, *Ḥunayn ibn Isḥāq on his Galen Translations*, p. 20.

of Galen's book on the *Causes*, it becomes clear that both the Alexandrian and Syriac scholars practiced that sort of critical engagement:

> This book is a miscellany in six volumes . . . Galen did not join all of these volumes into a single book, nor did he give them a single title. As for the Alexandrians, they joined them and called them *Causes*, a name derived from their major theme. As for the speakers of Syriac, they entitled them *Causes and Symptoms*. Such a title is not appropriate for the book and quite faulty. If they wanted to fill out the title, they ought to have added *and Diseases*.[141]

Adding New Thought to the Target Text

Creative engagement encompasses adding new information to the text by the translator. Although examples are abundant in all fields of translation, including medicine and philosophy, the most renowned example comes from the literature.[142] When ʿAbd Allāh ibn al-Muqaffaʿ (d. 759/60 CE) translated *Kalīla wa-Dimna*, he not only changed the title and rewrote the whole book in his beautiful Arabic style but he also became inspired and added his own stories to the book.

Kalīla wa-Dimna is a collection of the Indian fables of Bidpai, translated from intermediary Pahlavi, but originally written in Sanskrit under the title *Panchatantra*. Tarek Shamma analyzes *Kalīla wa-Dimna*, giving numerous examples of how Ibn al-Muqaffaʿ domesticated the text to its new Islamic context. Many words, phrases, and sentences that Ibn al-Muqaffaʿ integrated in his work are comparable to the Quranic terms and verses and are not, of course, part of the source text. Some Islamic concepts, such as the doctrine of reckoning on the Day of Judgment and the concept of *qadar* (destiny) that were introduced into the translation, play central roles.[143] In addition to these changes, Ibn al-Muqaffaʿ added his own original composition to the book. For example, the chapter entitled "*Al-faḥṣ ʿan amr Dimna*" (Investigating Dimna) was found neither in the original Sanskrit text nor in another old translation into Syriac. This chapter, in which Dimna is convicted and executed for manipulating the Lion into killing Shatraba, embodies the moral lesson of the story, and it is the chapter with the most Islamic character. It was added to secure a satisfactory response from the Muslim audience to the moral lesson of

141 Isḥāq, *Ḥunayn ibn Isḥāq on his Galen Translations*, p. 24.

142 The same analysis applies to *Alf Layla wa-layla* (*The Thousand and One Nights*), which combines Indian, Pahlavi, and Arabic elements. See Ulrich Marzolph. "Arabian Nights." In *Encyclopaedia of Islam*, edited by Kate Fleet, Gudrun Krämer, Denis Matringe, John Nawas, and Everett Rowson (Leiden: Brill, 2007).

143 Tarek Shamma. "Translating into the Empire: The Arabic Version of Kalila wa Dimna." *The Translator*, vol. 15, no. 1, 2009, pp. 65–86.

the book. According to Abd al-Wahhāb ʿAzzām, the Pahlavi version also had added chapters that did not exist in the Sanskrit version.[144]

Kalīla wa-Dimna played an important role in the development of Arabic literature, since prose narrative had not existed before in the Arabic literary system. Non-Arab converts to Islam who were raised in another culture like Ibn al-Muqaffaʿ thought that new literary genres such as the Indian fables might be admired by the Arabs, so Ibn al-Muqaffaʿ introduced *Kalīla wa-Dimna*, which was the first prose narrative in Arabic, and it paved the way for similar genres, such as the *maqāma* genre. Comparing *Kalīla wa-Dimna* and *al-Maqāmāt al-Luzūmiyya* of al-Saraquṣṭī (d. 538/1143 CE), David Wacks explains that:

> The two texts represent a convergence of different oral narrative traditions: in *Kalila*, we find the animal fable tradition originating in India, and in the *maqāma*, the Arabic tradition of popular preaching and story-telling, coupled with anecdotal religious literature such as the *hadīth*. The episodic frametale structure introduced into Arabic literature by *Kalīila* is adapted by the *maqāma*, which can be seen as one of Medieval literature's first forays into realistic prose fiction.[145]

Additions of new information in scientific and philosophical works are usually marked with a verbal phrase – for example, "Ḥunayn said" – attributing the new information to the translator. In her analysis of Galen's *Commentary on the Hippocratic Aphorisms* and its Arabic translation, Elaine van Dalen concludes that Ḥunayn uses the verb form *aḥsabu* ("I think," "I assume") sixteen times, "especially in the paragraphs in which he adds his own ideas to the translation." Another verb form that Ḥunayn uses frequently when adding his personal experience and thoughts to his translation is *najidu* ("we find").[146] This implies not only great respect to the source text but also a high regard for the moral responsibility of the translator. On the one hand, the translator does his best to produce an accurate and complete translation of the source text and marks his own additions and comments by introducing them with personal forms. On the other hand, the translator or scholar does not find it sufficient to convey the meaning of the source text without critically and creatively engaging with it. Further, similar to what the translator does to differentiate the original text from his additions, copyists, as with the manuscript of Ḥunayn's translation of Galen's commentaries on Hippocrates, sometimes write the introductory

---

144 Abd al-Wahhāb ʿAzzām. "Introduction." In *Kalīla wa-Dimna*, edited by Ṭāha Ḥusayn and Abd al-Wahhāb ʿAzzām (Cairo: Hindāwī, 1941).

145 David A. Wacks. "The Performativity of Ibn al-Muqaffaʿ's 'Kalīla wa-Dimna' and 'al-Maqāmāt al-Luzūmiyya' of al-Saraqusṭī." *Journal of Arabic Literature*, vol. 34, no. 1/2, 2003, p. 179.

146 Dalen, "Subjectivity in translation," pp. 72, 74.

formulae, such as "Ḥunayn said" and "Galen said," as well as the translator's notes, with different ink and in a thicker script.[147] This implies a high sense of moral responsibility on the part of copyists to differentiate between the original text and additions from the translator.

The following is an example of creative engagement from Ḥunayn's *Risāla*. In his comment on his translation of *Opinions of Hippocrates and Plato*, Ḥunayn explains that Job of Edessa translated that book into Syriac. Ḥunayn had several manuscripts of that book in Greek, so he worked on a new translation into Syriac. To that translation, he added a volume of his own "in defense of what Galen said in the seventh volume of this book."[148]

This practice of critically and creatively engaging with the source text would soon go beyond translation and pave the way for a whole tradition called *shukūk* (doubts). The first book in this genre was al-Rāzī's *Kitāb al-Shukūk ʿala Jālīnūs* (*The Book of Doubts Concerning Galen*). Al-Rāzī's criticisms of twenty-six books by Galen are not entirely different from Ḥunayn's critical and creative engagement with the Galenic corpus. Both corrected possible copyist errors, as well as information that was not consistent with Galen's ideas. In addition, they corrected information that was not consistent with their observation or experience.[149] Astronomical *shukūk* soon followed. As George Saliba says, the fact that the astronomical *shukūk* books were produced in al-Andalus, in the far Islamic West at that time, as well as in Bukhara, in the far Islamic East, and by astronomers as well as philosophers, "could only mean that the cosmological issues that were perceived to have plagued Ptolemaic astronomy were by then circulating in widespread intellectual and geographical circles; they were no longer restricted to the elite of astronomical theoreticians."[150] The *shukūk* genre was restricted neither to astronomy nor to the elite; it became a way of thinking and an approach to knowledge in general.

---

147 Vagelpohl, *Galeni In Hippocratis Epidemiarum Librum I Commentariorum I–III Versionem Arabicam/Galen*, p. 19.

148 Isḥāq, *Ḥunayn ibn Isḥāq on his Galen Translations*, p. 60.

149 Mahdī Muḥaqqiq, ed. *Kitāb al-Shukūk ʿalá Jālīnūs li-Muḥammad ibn Zakarīyā al-Rāzī* (Tehran: Mu'assasah-'i Muṭālaʿāt Islāmī, 1993).

150 Saliba, *Islamic Science and the Making of the European Renaissance*, p. 95.

7 A Model of Arabic Translation Analysis

A model for the analysis of medieval Arabic translation includes four processes: externalization, combination, internalization, and actualization. Externalization is the pouring of ideas into the world.[151] It applies to the production of knowledge that is contained in source texts produced prior to translation in another language and culture. However, it does not apply to translation as it is defined today, since it consists of old ideas expressed in a different language. The Greek texts that were translated into Arabic in the medieval age are instances of externalization, produced a long time before the Arabic translation movement.

Combination is the process of converting knowledge from the source language to the target language. This is the process through which groups and individuals combine knowledge, potentially creating new knowledge. I define translation, then, not as a process of knowledge transfer, but as a process of knowledge combination. In its simplest form, translation is a combination of two linguistic systems and two cultures. Linguistically speaking, when the ideas of the source text are expressed in another form (i.e. the target language), the translator does not produce a pure target text that is void of any influence of the language of the source text. There are usually traces of interference. However, even if this pure linguistic form is hypothetically achievable, we still have an instance of combination where ideas produced in another culture combine with a local linguistic system, thus being introduced to a new audience.

Combination may also occur at the level of content when the translator engages creatively with the source text. In the Arabic translation movement, we have more than one form of combination. For example, some Arabic translators, such as Ibrahim al-Fazārī, who translated *Zīj al-Sindhind al-Kabīr*, combine more than one source to produce their translations. When Ḥunayn ibn Isḥāq added a summary to some of his translations, he combined the full target text with his own perception of the more important information to include in a summary. Nevertheless, combination reaches a peak when translators add new thought to translation. In this case, they combine new knowledge, based on their expertise and environment, to knowledge that already exists in the source text. When Ibn al-Muqaffaʿ added fresh material to *Kalīla wa-Dimna*, he combined the Indian animal fables with his political project.

Since translation is both a process and a product, combination is observed in both. As a product, we can see new information integrated in the medieval Arabic translations, taking the form of glosses, commentaries, or text segments that were added. As a process, translation involves internalization and

[151] I borrow this definition from Berger, *The Sacred Canopy*.

actualization. Internalization means the translator comprehends the material of the source text fully enough that he can present it in a different form, such as writing a summary or adding new thoughts to it. Thus, internalization is a process of learning through translating. After internalizing the information of the source text, the translator begins to put his newly acquired knowledge to use, produces new knowledge, and adds it to the target text. In this sense, learning through translation is not only about knowing but also about becoming. Medieval Arabic translation is not repetition, imitation, or even participation in some pursuit totally designed by another culture; it is fusion that has created a new self. It is this new self that makes Arabic translation a prominent tradition. Iṣṭifan ibn Basīl was a superior example in this context. Iṣṭifan ibn Basīl did not sit with pen and paper and translate the source text. Between analyzing the source text and synthesizing the target text, he went through internalization and actualization. He studied the source text, learned about the drugs, administered them, and, after that, Arabized them.

Translation as a form of combination does not fully explain the success of the Abbasid translation movement because it is a process that was practiced only by the elite – the translators and scientists. Another aspect, which I call "the spiral of influence," explains the effect of translation on culture. This "spiral of influence" can explain how the medieval translation movement enriched the Arabic language. When a new term is introduced through translation, the masses who are actively engaged in learning begin to use it, so the term moves up the spiral until it becomes part of the Arabic language. Without the spiral of influence, the term remains in the narrow circles of the elite or it disappears. That is why translation needs a fertile learning environment to achieve its effect.

We have seen how translation in the Abbasid Golden Age introduced new ways of thinking and contributed to a more rational, critical, and creative frame of mind. Through a spiral of influence, the new way of thinking – along with the new terminology and tools of expression – involved more people from the public. This was facilitated by the fact that some translations were produced for the public, which accelerated the spiral of influence, speeding up the impact of translation on the masses. Once the circle of utilizing the products of translation was widened, new gaps began to appear. To close such gaps, more advanced knowledge in new translations or original compositions became a necessity, and so on and so forth.[152]

[152] This means that translation and original composition are simultaneous, not consecutive, processes. As George Saliba describes the Arabic translation movement, "some creative activities . . . preceded the translations of the advanced texts, and that those creative activities by themselves required further translations in order to lead to more creative thinking and so on" (Saliba, *Islamic Science and the Making of the European Renaissance*, p. 67).

8 How Arabic Translation Changed

In the medieval period, translation played a pivotal role at least twice in the progress of scientific knowledge. The first was the translation movement of Baghdad, when the works of the Greek masters were translated from Greek and intermediary Syriac into Arabic. The second was when the scholars of Toledo, the intellectual center of the Latin West, translated Arabic works into Latin. The Toledo translation movement featured characteristics from three sources: the Romans, the patristic writings, and the Arabic translation movement of Baghdad. The Arabic influence did not continue for long, and it was noticeable in only some of the early translations. The patristic views constituted the stronger influence on all religious and scientific translations, whereas the Roman approach of the rhetoricians was clear in literary translation.

With the advent of the Reformation in the sixteenth century and the challenges it posed to Catholicism, the Church grew suspicious of the effect of translation as an instrument for reinterpreting sacred texts, thus undermining the Church's authority as providing the "correct" interpretation. As a result, translation in general was discouraged, and greater formal fidelity and literalness was desired by churchmen to block interpretation, as well as by translators themselves to reduce any personal responsibility.[153] At the same time, the rise of philology and the increased interest in classical Latin confirmed that literalism is the best choice to rediscover the legacy of classical Latin and Greek literature.

In the history of Latin and vernacular European translation, literary translation is generally distinguished from sacred and scientific translation. Literary translation is concerned with the creation of new literary forms through translation, hence the idea of translation as creation, whereas sacred and scientific translations are concerned with the transmission of intellectual information. This was further emphasized in the nineteenth century, when literalism was the more widespread technique for scientific translation. In contrast, literary translation, particularly the translation of English Gothic novels into French, was responding to the entertainment demands of the market and, as a result, translators creatively carried out various changes such as inserting a totally new title, deleting whole passages, or adding fresh material to their translations.[154]

In late nineteenth-century Europe, philosophical and scientific works were no longer imported to Europe through translation, as Europe had become the source of original writings in these fields. Instead of philosophical and scientific

[153] Delisle and Woodsworth, *Translators through History*, pp. 134–8.
[154] Delisle and Woodsworth, *Translators through History*, p. 207.

works, "modernist translators were attracted to literary novelties."[155] There was a demand for literary translations to be made available soon after publications in the original language.

A similar market for literary translation emerged in the Middle East in the late nineteenth century; however, in the early nineteenth century through to the second half of the nineteenth century, there was a demand for scientific translation. That demand was represented by a strong translation movement in Egypt that emerged as a part of Muhammad Ali's modernizing project. As practiced within this translation movement, Arabic translation featured characteristics of both the Middle Age and the modern European translation practices. Like the Abbasid translators, the Arabic translators in Egypt engaged creatively with their source texts, but like the European translators, they gave priority to fluency and rhetorical style. Egypt, Syria, and Lebanon had a literary translation movement in the mid-nineteenth century, during which Arabic translation seemed to sever its ties with the Middle Ages and was fully influenced by the modern European translation theory and practice.

[155] Delisle and Woodsworth, *Translators through History*, p. 192.

References

ʿAzzām, Abd al-Wahhāb. "Introduction." In *Kalīla Wa-Dimna*, edited by Ṭāha Ḥusayn and Abd al-Wahhāb ʿAzzām (Cairo: Hindāwī, 1941).

Adamson, Peter. "Al-Kindī and the Reception of Greek Philosophy." In *The Cambridge Companion to Arabic Philosophy*, edited by Peter Adamson and Richard C. Taylor (Cambridge: Cambridge University Press, 2005), pp. 32–51.

al-Jabri, Muhammad Abed. *Al-Muṯaqqafūn Fī Al-Ḥadāra Al-ʿarabīya: Miḥnat Ibn Ḥanbal Wa-Nakbat Ibn Rušd* (Beirut: Markaz Dirāsāt al-Wiḥda al-ʿArabīya, 1995).

Al-Jubouri, Imad Al Din M. N. *History of Islamic Philosophy: With View of Greek Philosophy and Early History of Islam* (Hertford: Bright Pen, 2004).

Al-Nadīm, Ibn. *Al-Fahrist* (Beirut: Dār al-Miʿrifa, n.d.).

Al-Ṣafadī, Ṣalāḥ al-Din Khalīl ibn Aybak. *Al-Ghayth Al-Musajjam Fī Sharḥ Lāmiyyat Al-ʿAjam*. (Syria, n.d.).

Aly, El-Hussein A. Y. *Qurʾān Translation as a Modern Phenomenon* (Leiden: Brill, 2023).

Amīn, Aḥmad. *Ḍuḥā Al-ʿIslām* (Cairo: Hindawi Foundation for Education and Culture, 2011).

Awni, Muhammad Abdelraouf. *Tārīkh Al-Tarjama Al-ʿArabiyya Bayna Al-Sharq Al-ʿArabi Wa Al-Gharb Al-ʾŪrubi*, 2nd ed. (Cairo: Adāb, 2012).

Bäck, Allan. "Avicenna the Commentator." In *Medieval Commentaries on Aristotle's Categories*, edited by Lloyd Newton (Leiden: Brill, 2008), pp. 31–71.

Baker, Mona. "Arabic Tradition." In *Routledge Encyclopedia of Translation Studies*, edited by Mona Baker (London: Routledge, 2001), pp. 316–25.

Barkhudarov, Leonid. "The Problem of the Unit of Translation." In *Translation as Social Action: Russian and Bulgarian Perspectives*, edited by Palma Zlateva and Andre Lefevere (London: Routledge, 1993), pp. 39–46.

Basalamah, Salah. "The Notion of Translation in the Arab World: A Critical Developmental Perspective." In *A World Atlas of Translation*, edited by Yves Gambier and Ubaldo Stecconi (Amsterdam: John Benjamins, 2019), pp. 169–92.

Bassnett, Susan. "Translation and Ideology." *Koiné, Annali della Scuola Superiore per Interpreti e Traduttori "San Pellegrino"*, vol. 1, no. 2, 1991, pp. 7–32.

Bell, Roger T. *Translation and Translating: Theory and Practice* (New York: Longman, 1991).

Berger, Peter L. *The Sacred Canopy: Elements of a Sociological Theory of Religion* (New York: Open Road Integrated Media, 2011).

Bhabha, Homi K. *The Location of Culture* (London: Routledge, 1994).

Burnett, Charles. "Arabic into Latin: The Reception of Arabic Philosophy into Western Europe." In *The Cambridge Companion to Arabic Philosophy*, edited by Peter Adamson and Richard C. Taylor (Cambridge: Cambridge University Press, 2005), pp. 370–90.

Cooper, Glen M. "Ḥunayn Ibn Isḥāq and the Creation of an Arabic Galen." In *Brill's Companion to the Reception of Galen*, edited by Petros Bouras-Vallianatos and Barbara Zipser (Leiden: Brill, 2019), pp. 179–95.

D'ancona, Cristina. "Greek into Arabic: Neoplatonism in Translation." In *The Cambridge Companion to Arabic Philosophy*, edited by Peter Adamson and Richard C. Taylor (Cambridge: Cambridge University Press, 2005), pp. 10–31.

Delabastita, Dirk. "Continentalism and the Invention of Traditions in Translation Studies." In *Eurocentrism in Translation Studies*, edited by Luc van Doorslaer and Peter Flynn (Amsterdam: John Benjamins, 2013), pp. 29–42.

Delisle, Jean, and Judith Woodsworth. *Translators through History* (Amsterdam: John Benjamins, 1995).

Even-Zohar, Itamar. "Polysystem Studies." *Poetics Today*, vol. 11, no. 1, 1990, pp. 9–26.

Filius, Lourus S. *The Arabic Version of Aristotle's Historia Animalium: Book I–X of Kitāb Al-Hayawān* (Leiden: Brill, 2018).

Fiori, Emiliano. "Sergius of Reshaina and Pseudo-Dionysius: A Dialectical Fidelity." In *Interpreting the Bible and Aristotle in Late Antiquity: The Alexandrian Commentary Tradition between Rome and Baghdad*, edited by Josef Lössl and John Watt (Farnham, UK: Ashgate, 2011), pp. 180–94.

"Sergius of Resh'aynā." In *Encyclopedia of Medieval Philosophy*, edited by Henrik Lagerlund (Dordrecht: Springer Netherlands, 2011), pp. 1185–8.

Gentzler, Edwin. "Macro- and Micro-Turns in Translation Studies." In *Eurocentrism in Translation Studies*, edited by Luc van Doorslaer and Peter Flynn (Amsterdam: John Benjamins, 2013), pp. 9–28.

Translation and Identity in the Americas: New Directions in Translation Theory (London: Routledge, 2008).

Gottheil, Richard, and Max Schloessinger. "Masarjawaih or Masarjoyah or Masarjis." In *Jewish Encyclopedia*. www.jewishencyclopedia.com/articles/10458-masarjawaih.

Grant, Edward. *A Source Book in Medieval Science* (Cambridge, MA: Harvard University Press, 1974).

Gutas, Dimitri. *Greek Thought, Arabic Culture: The Graeco-Arabic Translation Movement in Baghdad and Early ʿAbbāsid Society (2nd–4th/8th–10th Centuries)* (New York: Routledge, 1998).

Hallum, Bink. "The Arabic Reception of Galen's *Commentary on Hippocrates' 'Epidemics'*." In *Epidemics in Context: Greek Commentaries on Hippocrates in the Arabic Tradition*, edited by Peter E. Pormann (Berlin: De Gruyter, 2012), pp. 185–210.

Haq, Syed Nomanul. "The Indian and Persian Background." In *History of Islamic Philosophy*, edited by Seyyed Hossein Nasr and Oliver Leaman (London: Routledge, 1996), pp. 52–70.

Hodgson, Marshall G. S. *The Venture of Islam, Volume 2: The Expansion of Islam in the Middle Periods* (Chicago, IL: University of Chicago Press, 2009).

House, Juliana. *A Model for Translation Quality Assessment* (Tübingen: Gunter Narr Verlag, 1977).

Ibn Abī Uṣaibiʿa, Aḥmad. *A Literary History of Medicine: The 'Uyūn Al-Anbā' Fī Ṭabaqāt Al-Aṭibbāʾ of Ibn Abī Uṣaybiʾah*, translated by Emilie Savage-Smith, Simon Swain, Geert Jan H. van Gelder, I. J. S. Rojo, N. P. Joosse, A. Watson, B. Inksetter, and F. Hilloowala (Leiden: Brill, 2020).

Uyūn Al-Anbāʾ Fī Ṭabaqāt Al-Aṭibbāʾ (Cairo: Al-Wahbiyya, 1882).

Isḥāq, Ḥunayn ibn. *Ḥunayn Ibn Isḥāq on His Galen Translations*, edited and translated by John C. Lamoreaux (Provo, UT: Brigham Young University Press, 2016).

Risālat Ḥunayn ibn Isḥāq (Iran: Muṭalaʿāte Islāmi, 1949).

Krings, Hans P. *Repairing Texts: Empirical Investigations of Machine Translation Post-Editing Processes*, edited by Geoffrey S. Koby (Kent, OH: The Kent State University Press, 2001).

Lohr, Charles. H. "The Medieval Interpretation of Aristotle." In *The Cambridge History of Later Medieval Philosophy*, edited by Norman Kretzmann, Anthony Kenny, and Jan Pinborg (Cambridge: Cambridge University Press, 2008), pp. 80–91.

Lössl, Josef, and John Watt. "Introduction." In *Interpreting the Bible and Aristotle in Late Antiquity: The Alexandrian Commentary Tradition between Rome and Baghdad*, edited by Josef Lössl and John Watt (Farnham, UK: Ashgate, 2011), pp. 1–10.

Marzolph, Ulrich. "Arabian Nights." In *Encyclopaedia of Islam*, edited by Kate Fleet, Gudrun Krämer, Denis Matringe, John Nawas, and Everett Rowson (Leiden: Brill, 2007).

Mattock, John N. "The Early Translations from Greek into Arabic: An Experiment in Comparative Assessment." *Symposium Graeco-Arabicum II: Akten des Zweiten Symposium Graeco-Arabicum, Ruhr-Universität Bochum*, vols. 2 1989, pp. 73–102.

McCollum, Adam. "Sergius of Reshaina as Translator: The Case of the De Mundo." In *Interpreting the Bible and Aristotle in Late Antiquity: The Alexandrian Commentary Tradition between Rome and Baghdad*, edited by Josef Lössl and John Watt (Farnham, UK: Ashgate, 2011), pp. 165–78.

Mitchell, Timothy. *Colonising Egypt* (Cambridge: Cambridge University Press, 1988).

Montgomery, Scott. *Science in Translation: Movements of Knowledge through Cultures and Time* (Chicago: University of Chicago Press, 2000).

Morrison, Robert. "Astronomy." In *Medieval Islamic Civilization: An Encyclopedia*, edited by Joseph Meri and Jere Bacharach (London: Routledge, 2006).

Muḥaqqiq, Mahdī, ed. *Kitāb Al-Shukūk 'alá Jālīnūs Li-Muḥammad Ibn Zakarīyā Al-Rāzī* (Tehran: Mu'assasah-'i Muṭāla'āt Islāmī, 1993).

Newmark, Peter. *A Textbook of Translation* (New York: Prentice-Hall International, 1988).

Olohan, Maeve. *Scientific and Technical Translation* (London: Routledge, 2015).

Pormann, Peter E. "The Development of Translation Techniques from Greek into Syriac and Arabic: The Case of Galen's On the Faculties and Powers of Simple Drugs, Book Six." In *Medieval Arabic Thought: Essays in Honour of Fritz Zimmermann*, edited by Rotraud E. Hansberger, Muhammad A. al-Akiti, Charles S. F. Burnett, and Fritz W. Zimmermann (London: Warburg Institute, 2012), pp. 143–62.

Rigolio, Alberto. "Aristotle's Poetics in Syriac and in Arabic Translations: Readings of 'Tragedy'." *Khristianskii Vostok*, vol. 6, 2013, pp. 140–9.

Rosenthal, Franz. *The Classical Heritage in Islam Arabic Thought and Culture* (London: Routledge, 2005).

Salama-Carr, Myriam. "Medieval Translators into Arabic – Scribes or Interpreters?" In *Beyond the Western Tradition*, edited by Marilyn Gaddis Rose (New York: State University of New York at Binghamton), pp. 99–105.

Salama-Carr, Myriam, and Theo Hermans. "Translation into Arabic in the 'Classical' Age: When the Pandora's Box of Transmission Opens." *Translating Others*, vol. 1, 2006, pp. 121–31.

Saliba, George. *Islamic Science and the Making of the European Renaissance* (Cambridge, MA: MIT Press, 2007).

Shamma, Tarek. "Translating into the Empire: The Arabic Version of Kalila Wa Dimna." *The Translator*, vol. 15, no. 1, 2009, pp. 65–86.

Strohmaier, Gotthard. "Galen the Pagan and Ḥunayn the Christian: Specific Transformations in the Commentaries on *Airs, Waters, Places* and the *Epidemics*." In *Epidemics in Context: Greek Commentaries on Hippocrates in the Arabic Tradition*, edited by Peter E. Pormann (Berlin: De Gruyter, 2012), pp. 171–84.

Toury, Gideon. *In Search of a Theory of Translation* (Tel Aviv: Porter Institute for Poetics and Semiotics, Tel Aviv University, 1980).

Vagelpohl, Uwe. *Aristotle's Rhetoric in the East: The Syriac and Arabic Translation and Commentary Tradition* (Leiden: Brill, 2008).

"Galen, *Epidemics*, Book One: Text, Transmission, Translation." In *Epidemics in Context: Greek Commentaries on Hippocrates in the Arabic Tradition*, edited by Peter E. Pormann (Berlin: De Gruyter, 2012), pp. 125–50.

Galeni in Hippocratis Epidemiarum Librum I Commentariorum I–III Versionem Arabicam/Galen. Commentary on Hippocrates' Epidemics Book I: Edidit, in Linguam Anglicam Vertit, Commentatus Est (Berlin: De Gruyter, 2014).

"The Abbasid Translation Movement in Context: Contemporary Voices on Translation." In *Abbasid Studies II. Occasional Papers of the School of Abbasid Studies. Leuven, 28 June–1 July 2004*, edited by John Nawas (Leuven: Peeters, 2010), pp. 245–67.

"The User-Friendly Galen: Ḥunayn Ibn Isḥāq and the Adaptation of Greek Medicine for a New Audience." In *Greek Medical Literature and Its Readers: From Hippocrates to Islam and Byzantium*, edited by Petros Bouras-Vallianatos and Sophia Xenophontos (London: Routledge, 2018), pp. 113–31.

Vagelpohl, Uwe, and Ignacio Sanchez. "Why Do We Translate? Arabic Sources on Translation." In *Why Translate Science*, edited by Dimitri Gutas (Leiden: Brill, 2022), pp. 254–376.

van Dalen, Elaine. "Subjectivity in Translation: Ḥunayn Ibn Isḥāq's Ninth-Century Interpretation of Galen's 'Ego' in His *Commentary on the Hippocratic Aphorisms*." *Oriens*, vol. 45, 2017, pp. 53–79.

van Doorslaer, Luc. "(More Than) American Prisms on Eurocentrisms: An Interview Article." In *Eurocentrism in Translation Studies*, edited by Luc van Doorslaer and Peter Flynn (Amsterdam: John Benjamins, 2013), pp. 113–21.

Wacks, David A. "The Performativity of Ibn Al-Muqaffaʿ's 'Kalīla Wa-Dimna' and 'Al-Maqāmāt Al-Luzūmiyya' of Al-Saraqusṭī." *Journal of Arabic Literature*, vol. 34, no. 1/2, 2003, pp. 178–89.

Walzer, Richard. *Greek into Arabic: Essays on Islamic Philosophy* (Cambridge, MA: Harvard University Press, 1962).

"New Light on the Arabic Translations of Aristotle." *Oriens*, vol. 6, no. 1, 1953, pp. 91–142.

Watt, John. "From Sergius to Mattā: Aristotle and Pseudo-Dionysius in the Syriac Tradition." In *Interpreting the Bible and Aristotle in Late Antiquity: The Alexandrian Commentary Tradition between Rome and Baghdad*, edited by Josef Lössl and John Watt (Farnham, UK: Ashgate, 2011), pp. 239–57.

Wright, Sue Ellen, and Leland D. Wright, Jr., eds. *Scientific and Technical Translation* (Amsterdam: John Benjamins, 1993).

Cambridge Elements

Translation and Interpreting

The series is edited by Kirsten Malmkjær with Sabine Braun as associate editor for Elements focusing on Interpreting.

Kirsten Malmkjær

University of Leicester

Kirsten Malmkjær is Professor Emeritus of Translation Studies at the University of Leicester. She has taught Translation Studies at the universities of Birmingham, Cambridge, Middlesex and Leicester and has written extensively on aspects of both the theory and practice of the discipline. *Translation and Creativity* (London: Routledge) was published in 2020 and *The Cambridge Handbook of Translation*, which she edited, was published in 2022. She is preparing a volume entitled *Introducing Translation* for the Cambridge Introductions to Language and Linguistics series.

Sabine Braun

University of Surrey

Sabine Braun is Professor of Translation Studies and Director of the Centre for Translation Studies at the University of Surrey. She is a world-leading expert on interpreting and on research into human and machine interaction in translation and interpreting, for example to improve access to information, media and public services for linguistic-minority populations and other groups/people in need of communication support. She has written extensively on these topics, including *Videoconference and Remote Interpreting in Criminal Proceedings*, with J. Taylor, 2012; Here or There: Research on Interpreting via Video Link, with J. Napier and R. Skinner, 2018; and *Innovation in Audio Description Research*, with K. Starr, 2020.

About the Series

Elements in Translation and Interpreting present cutting edge studies on the theory, practice and pedagogy of translation and interpreting. The series also features work on machine learning and AI, and human-machine interaction, exploring how they relate to multilingual societies with varying communication and accessibility needs, as well as text-focused research.

Cambridge Elements

Translation and Interpreting

Elements in the Series

Translation and Genre
B. J. Woodstein

Translation as Experimentalism: Exploring Play in Poetics
Tong King Lee

On-Screen Language in Video Games
Mikołaj Deckert and Krzysztof Hejduk

Navigating the Web
Claire Y Shih

The Graeco-Arabic Translation Movement
El-Hussein A. Y. Aly

A full series listing is available at: www.cambridge.org/EITI

Printed in the United States
by Baker & Taylor Publisher Services